Bredon Church

THE OLD PARISH CHURCHES
OF WORCESTERSHIRE

Mike Salter

FOLLY PUBLICATIONS

ACKNOWLEDGEMENTS

The photographs and measured drawings in this book are the product of the author's fieldwork between 1971 and 1995. Old postcards and brass rubbings are reproduced from originals in the the author's collection. Thanks are due to Max Barfield for providing word processor facilities, checking the text, and the loan of a camera.

ABOUT THIS BOOK

This book is a much extended and revised new edition with extra plans and photographs of a 76 page book originally released in 1989 and reprinted in 1993. As with the other books about churches in this series (see the full list on the inside of the back cover) it concentrates on the period prior to the Industrial Revolution of the late 18th century. Most furnishings and monuments after 1770 are not mentioned, although additions and alterations to the fabric usually are, although in less detail. New churches of after 1770 are not mentioned in the gazetteer, nor do they appear on the map. They are, however, listed towards the back of this edition.

The book is inevitably very much a catalogue of dates and names, etc. It is intended as a field guide and for reference rather than to be read from cover to cover. Occasionally there is a comment about the setting of a church but on the whole little is said about their position or atmosphere. The amount of material given for a particular church in this book is not necessarily a true indication of how interesting or attractive the building may be. Interesting and attractive features of the churches and their graveyards may lie outside the scope of the book. Visit them and judge for yourself. The gazetteer features Ordnance Survey grid references (these are the two letters and six digits which appears after each place-name and dedication) and the book is intended to be used in conjunction with 1:50,000 scale maps.

Plans redrawn from originals in the author's field notebooks are reproduced to a common scale of 1:400. The buildings were measured in metres and only metric scales are given. A system of hatching common to all the plans is used to denote the different periods of work. The plans should be treated with care and cross-referenced with the text, as there are some things that are difficult to convey on a small scale plan such as dressed stones of one period being reset or reused in a later period.

ABOUT THE AUTHOR

Mike Salter is 41 and has been a professional writer and publisher since he went on the Government Enterprise Allowance Scheme for unemployed people in 1988. He is particularly interested in the planning and layout of medieval buildings and has a huge collection of plans of churches and castles he has measured during tours (mostly by bicycle and motorcycle) of England, Ireland, Scotland and Wales since 1968. Wolverhampton born and bred, Mike now lives in an old cottage beside the Malvern Hills. His other interests include walking, model railways, board games, morris dancing, folk music, and he plays a variety of percussion instruments.

ISBN 1 871731 24 0

Chaddesley Corbett Church

CONTENTS

Inside the front cover is a map of churches in the gazetteer.

INTRODUCTION

The district which later came to be the county of Worcester (amalgamated with the county of Hereford in 1974) was converted to Christianity by the mid 7th century. The monastic cathedral of Worcester existed by 680, and other abbeys were founded at Pershore and Evesham in c689 and 714. Until the 16th century these establishments, plus a few others, notably the priory of Great Malvern founded c1085, dominated life in the county and diocese (which covered roughly the same area). The church held a high proportion of the land in Worcestershire and in the 13th century the patronage of 84 parishes out of the then total of 115 was in the hands of the Bishop and the heads of the four great monasteries mentioned above.

The Domesday Book of 1086 records Worcestershire as having 60 priests at 57 places which were mostly in the south of the county. This means that the county contained over 50 parish churches in the Saxon period, but no structural remains exist of any of them. Many were undoubtedly humble structures of wood, and those buildings which were of stone must have been rebuilt and extended in later centuries to the point that the original buildings ceased to exist. The only relics of the Saxon period are the 9th century cross head at Cropthorne, a few fragments of crosses with interlace at Frankley, Rous Lench, and Stoke Prior, and a part of a tombstone at the mansion of Severn End in the parish of Hanley Castle.

As in most parts of England, work of the period 1066-1120 is sparse in ordinary parish churches in Worcestershire, although Worcester Cathedral has a crypt of the 1080s, Pershore Abbey a transept of c1100, and Great Malvern Priory arcades perhaps of the 1120s. The chancel at Elmley Castle with herringbone masonry may be 11th century while Cropthorne has an early 12th century arcade. Other minor work which may possibly be this early elsewhere is not of much importance.

Norman work at Astley

Herringbone masonry at Elmley Castle

Norman arcades at Cropthorne

Nearly half of the 185 churches described in the gazetteer have work remaining from the period 1130-1200 when many new churches were built so that most people did not have far to travel to worship. In some cases only a re-positioned doorway or font has survived subsequent rebuilding, but there are many instances in Worcestershire where the remains of that period are extensive and impressive. The county has remained largely pastoral with only a modest population growth and as a result about a third of the churches have never required the addition of aisles to accommodate an increased congregation.

Most 12th century churches had a rectangular nave for the congregation with a round arch in the east wall opening into a smaller compartment called a chancel which was often only just big enough to contain an altar and attendant clergy. The much more spacious chancels with space to take a singing choir were a later development. The nave usually has a doorway and two or three small windows set high up in each of the north and south walls, and either a doorway or another window in the west wall, all the openings being round headed. Stoulton has a fairly spacious and complete church of this type of c1130-40 with flat pilaster buttresses on the outside wall faces, a typical Norman feature. This building, and a group of others in the valley of the River Teme, have doorways set in projecting pieces of walling, and at Eastham, Bockleton, Knighton, and Stoulton there is blank arcading over the doorway. These doorways have sculptured motifs of a bold and simple kind such as heavy roll-mouldings and cross patterns. Ribbesford, Romsley, and Rochford each have sculptured tympanums of c1140-50 set over square-headed doorways, whilst Rous Lench has a very fine carving of a Christ in Majesty of about the same period.

Sculptural detail becomes more complex in the late 12th century and there are fine displays of c1160-75 at Holt and Rock with arches heavily ornamented with the chevron or zig-zag motif first used a generation earlier. At Cropthorne and Fladbury the lower parts of the west towers are of c1180, whilst those of Harvington and Tenbury Wells are of c1190-1200. Beckford has a central tower and there are remains of another at Pirton, whilst Powick has late 12th century transepts. There are arcades of c1150-60 at Cropthorne, Chaddesley Corbett and Overbury, and arcades of the end of the 12th century at Rous Lench, Eckington, Clent, Leigh, Pershore, Chaddesley Corbet, and St Alban and St John at Worcester.

Almost all the parochial churches, and the many chapels-of-ease which later attained parochial status, existed by 1200. In most cases the later medieval centuries only needed to make occasional repairs and add towers, aisles, porches, more spacious chancels, and to insert larger new windows as required. The east end of Pershore Abbey church is a major work of the first third of the 13th century. About forty of the ordinary parish churches have 13th century portions, including nine towers and twenty chancels, but little of the work is of much importance. Exceptions are the aisled nave at Ripple, the north transeptal tower of St Andrew at Droitwich, and the chancels at Bockleton, Beckford, Kempsey, and Overbury, the last having a rib vault. Hill Croome and Clifton-on-Teme churches are mostly of this period, and there are modest aisles at Throckmorton and Stoke Bliss. Several other aisles of this period exist, but only in a rather more altered and rebuilt condition.

Towards the end of the 13th century the simple Early English style developed into the generally more florid mature Gothic style known as Decorated. The west towers at Longdon and Upton-upon-Severn, the north transeptal tower at Severn Stoke, and the central tower and much else at Throckmorton date from c1300 and introduce us to this era. Again there is not much of importance apart from the central tower, north aisle and chancel at Bredon, the chancel at Chaddesley Corbett, the south chapel at Broadwas, the transept, aisle, and chancel at Severn Stoke, and the single-bodied church at Sedgeberrow with an octagonal west tower. Also of this period are considerable parts of the churches at Strensham, Birtsmorton, Hadzor, and Abbots Morton, aisles at Powick and Fladbury, the chancel at Harvington, and the south porch-towers at Hampton Lovett and Arley Kings. There are in all twenty church towers of the 14th century in Worcestershire, that at Bredon having a stone spire.

Bretforton Church

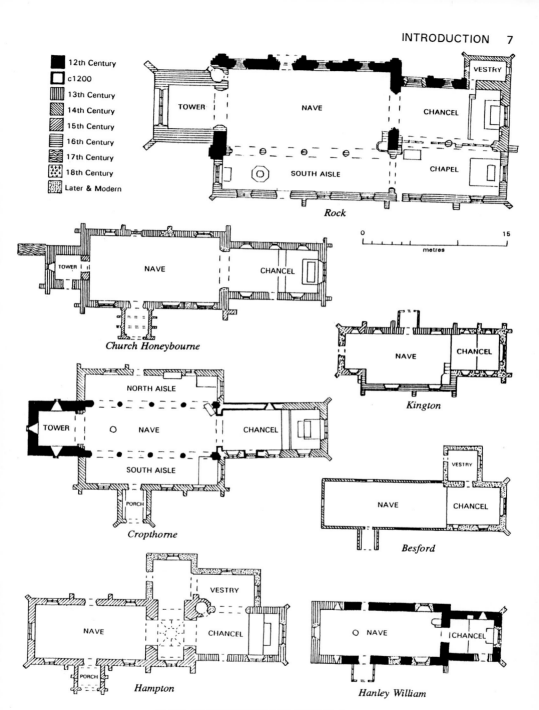

12th Century
c1200
13th Century
14th Century
15th Century
16th Century
17th Century
18th Century
Later & Modern

TOWER
NAVE
CHANCEL
VESTRY
SOUTH AISLE
CHAPEL

Rock

0   15
metres

TOWER
NAVE
CHANCEL

Church Honeybourne

NAVE
CHANCEL

Kington

NORTH AISLE
TOWER
NAVE
CHANCEL
SOUTH AISLE
PORCH

Cropthorne

VESTRY
NAVE
CHANCEL

Besford

NAVE
VESTRY
CHANCEL
PORCH

Hampton

NAVE
CHANCEL

Hanley William

PLANS OF SEVEN WORCESTERSHIRE CHURCHES

After the middle of the 14th century the Decorated stye slowly changed into the less fussy Perpendicular style, so called because of a tendency to emphasise verticals. This style remained in vogue until the Reformation of the 1530s. In Worcestershire churches the style begins with the new arcades at Powick, and the inserted new central tower at Broadway of c1380-1400. The chief building in the style in Worcestershire is Great Malvern Priory church as rebuilt c1420-60. This building is all-embattled and covered with decorative blank panelling, a motif also used on the upper stage of the central tower at Little Malvern Priory Church, and on the tower arches at Powick and Kempsey. Nearly every medieval church has some work of this period even if only a large new window or two. Several naves were provided with rows of clerestory windows over the arcades, and there are over forty towers including those of Cleeve Prior, Eldersfield, and St Andrew and St John at Worcester. Other towers at Overbury and Hampton are placed between the nave and chancel rather than at the more usual position of the west end. North Claines, Inkberrow, and Kidderminster churches are mostly of c1480-1520. Kidderminster (mostly refaced in the 19th century) has extreme length because of the placing of what was originally a detached Lady Chapel beyond the chancel. Rock has a south aisle with a chapel beyond it and a tower all of c1510. Church Honeybourne and Hampton have stone roofed porches, whilst Leigh has a timber west porch in front of a tower of c1380. Newly constructed 15th century aisles are not common in Worcestershire. Apart from the examples already noted, Ribbesford is the only country church showing much sign of expansion in this period, but considerable extensions were carried out to the town churches at Worcester, Evesham, and Pershore.

Worcestershire has quite a number of timber framed structures remaining in the fabric of its parish churches. None of those are likely to be older than c1300, but they form a reminder that quite a lot of churches and chapels as first built were timber framed. Rarities are the 14th century nave at Besford with lozenge panels and the aisled tower at Pirton. Cotheridge, Dormston, and Warndon also have timber framed towers, while Defford has a timber framed upper stage set on a stone lower stage. Ribbesford has an arcade of timber posts, St Peter's at Droitwich has a timber clerestory, and Crowle, Pendock, Huddington, and Romsley have timber framed porches of note.

All Saints, Evesham

Sedgeberrow Church

St Martin's Church, Worcester

Clifton-upon-Teme, 13th century

Hampton, c1400

Croome D'Abitot, 1760s

Great Malvern, late 15th century

Dormston, 15th century

WORCESTERSHIRE CHURCH TOWERS

English parish churches have many furnishings, monuments and roofs of the period 1550-1700 but little structural work apart from the occasional tower, porch, chapel, or repair job. There are chapels at Beoley, Mamble, and Hampton Lovett, towers at Hartlebury and Shrawley, and an aisle at Himbleton which are late 16th century. Of the 17th century are the chapels at Little Comberton, Cotheridge, Spetchley, the chancel at Ashton-under-Hill, towers at Wickhamford and Alvechurch, and major work comprising a central tower, chapel, and chancel all of brick (and dated 1674). All these have debased Gothic features but the slender tower of the 1690s at Bewdley features the Classical forms then becoming fashionable.

Worcester was a prosperous town in the 18th century and has four Classical style 18th century churches having wide naves with or without arcades, west towers, and shallow chancels. These are St Nicholas, c1730-35, St Swithun, 1734-36, All Saints, 1739-42, and St Martin, 1768-72. New churches were added to older towers at Bewdley in 1745-48, and Upton-upon-Severn in 1756-7, although little now remains of the latter. More important than any of these is the church at Great Witley, plain outside but with a Baroque interior unsurpassed in Britain. Broome is a much more modest country church of this era. There are 18th century towers added to older churches at Chaddesley Corbett, Frankley, Upper Arley, Dodderhill, and Bockleton. The churches of the 1760s and 70s at Croome D'Abitot, Stanford-on-Teme, Wolverley, and Tardbigge take us up to the time of the Industrial Revolution and the mark the end of the period covered in detail in this book.

17th century chancel at Ashton-under-Hill

Doorways and masonry styles can help to date the different parts of churches, but usually the outline shape of the windows and the tracery they contain is the best evidence, although it should be remembered that windows can be older or younger than the walling into which they are set. During the 12th century windows gradually increased in size from the tiny round headed windows of the Saxon and Early Norman periods to the long lancet windows with pointed heads which appear around 1200. Plain Norman windows are very common in Worcestershire. Windows with side-shafts start to appear c1160 as at Rock, and there are windows of the 1190s with two round arched lights under a round head in the towers at Harvington and Tenbury Wells.

Small pointed lancets can be seen at Broadwas, and longer ones at Clifton-on-Teme and Cleeve Prior. Tall pairs of lancets dating from c1250 occur in the chancels at Kempsey and Beckford. The east window at Beckford illustrates the next development, for it has three lancets with tiny circles pierced through the spandrels between the heads of the lights. By the 1260s pairs of lights with trefoiled heads appeared at Bredon and Bockleton, and at Church Honeybourne there are single light windows of c1290 with a trefoil set under a plain pointed outer arch. Of c1300 are numerous windows with two lights with a mullion which forks into two at the top, producing what is called Y-tracery. The same idea used in a window of more than two lights produces intersecting tracery, as at Bromsgrove, where there is also a development on this theme with the lights under the Y cusped and a quatrefoil set above.

The east window of c1320 at Chaddesley Corbett is an example of the more exuberant forms of tracery from which the Decorated style takes its name. A simpler version of the same style appears in the chapel windows of c1340 at Broadwas, while typical two light types of window based on the Y-tracery type but using the newly adopted ogival arch can be seen at Harvington and Stoke Prior. The latter has another typical Decorated form, reticulated or net-like tracery, while the chancel at Bredon illustrates earlier (c1310) pre-ogee tracery.

In Worcestershire parish churches the Decorated style merges almost imperceptively with the new Perpendicular style in the late 14th century. The east window of c1400 at Little Comberton has the unbroken mullions typical of the Perpendicular style but typical Decorated shapes forming the subdivisions. Cotheridge has a good 15th century south window with complex tracery and other good windows of c1450-70 can be seen at Castlemorton and North Claines. At both these churches the windows have four-centred heads which require four compass points to draw their shape. North Claines also has windows with square heads and this form was used for the continuous rows of clerestory windows at Upper Arley and Kidderminster which produce the glasshouse effect fashionable in this period.

17th Century (right) & Victorian windows at Hanley Castle

South Littleton Church

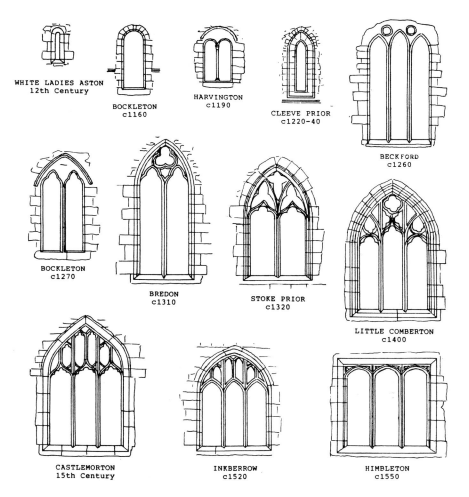

WHITE LADIES ASTON
12th Century

BOCKLETON
c1160

HARVINGTON
c1190

CLEEVE PRIOR
c1220-40

BECKFORD
c1260

BOCKLETON
c1270

BREDON
c1310

STOKE PRIOR
c1320

LITTLE COMBERTON
c1400

CASTLEMORTON
15th Century

INKBERROW
c1520

HIMBLETON
c1550

CHURCH WINDOWS IN WORCESTERSHIRE

After 1500 cusping is sometimes dispensed with as in the west window at Rock and the north aisle at Inkberrow. Tracery becomes simpler, then disappears also, as in the chapel east window at Hampton Lovett. By the Elizabethan period lights have round heads instead of four-centred ones. Single windows with several round arched lights set under a square head then remained in fashion well into the 17th century.

In the 1720s large round headed classical style windows without tracery appear in the church at Great Whitley. This church was closely followed by several at Worcester and that at Bewdley which has a large Venetian east window with square headed lights set either side off a higher round headed one. The Victorians experimented with all the older styles and examples of their era occur frequently in the churches that they restored.

Between 1840 and 1914 most of the old parish churches in Worcestershire were restored and refurnished. Some had become neglected and a few needed enlarging to accommodate an increased congregation or required the luxury of a new porch or vestry, but many were renovated as much for the sake of fashion as much as anything else. The medieval fabric of the churches in Worcestershire survived rather better than in some counties (such as Staffordshire), but nevertheless many ancient architectural features were obliterated, medieval furnishings replaced, and quite a number of monuments, especially brasses and incised slabs, were lost.

Fonts of the period 1130-1200 are common in Worcestershire and there are about two dozen with ornamentation of some kind, usually a rope moulding, a plait, chevrons, or blank arches, as at Broome, Pinvin, and Stoke Bliss, while Pershore also has seated figures. Medallions showing the Lamb and Cross occur at Rock, Inkberrow, and Bricklehampton, and others have rosettes. Chaddesley Corbet has a fine font with four dragons, and there are also four dragons, this time depicted more fully three dimensionally, around the base of the 13th century font at Elmley Castle. The few other 13th century and 14th century fonts in the county are unimportant. Fonts of the 15th century are more frequent and there is a small group dating from the 1660s.

Miserichord at Ripple

Easter Sepulchre at Bredon

In the later medieval period it became customary for the chancel of a church to be divided off from the nave by a screen with a Rood or image of the crucifixion fixed over it. Sometimes there was a loft over the screen for the use of musicians and the performers of religious plays. Other screens divided off side chapels and transepts. In the medieval period priests would chant masses in Latin which could not be understood by most of the congregation. At the Reformation many screens were ripped out because of the idols mounted upon them and because services in the chancel could hardly be heard by the congregation in the nave. Other screens were removed during 19th century restorations. Sometimes the steps up to the former loft still remain, and carved fragments from chancel screens sometimes appear reused in altar rails, pulpits, pews and tower screens. About a dozen late medieval chancel screens survive partly or wholly in Worcestershire. Probably the best is that at Shelsley Walsh, and others are at Leigh, Queenhill, and Salwarpe.

Medieval pulpits are rare as long sermons only became fashionable in the 16th century. A 15th century specimen survives at Grafton Flyford but the majority of pre-19th century pulpits are of c1610-40. That at Cotheridge is a typical example. Medieval doors survive here and there and there are many instances of medieval ironwork being reset on a more recent door. Communion rails of the late 16th, 17th, and 18th centuries are quite common. Many churches have 15th century tiles, especially around the high altar at the chancel east end and there is a unique set of medieval wall tiles at Great Malvern. The same church is also pre-eminent for medieval stained glass, having a complete set of windows of c1460-1500, while Great Witley has some remarkable 18th century glass. About three dozen other churches have 14th or 15th century glass, but mostly only small fragments sometimes not in their original setting. Stalls fitted with miserichords (hinged seats having lips to give support to standing choristers) remain at Ripple and Great Malvern, and bench ends, in some cases with early 16th century linenfold panels, remain at several other places. A few churches retain iron bound wooden chests in which the plate was secured. Crowle and Norton have rare 12th century stone lecterns.

Jacobean pulpit at Cotheridge

Font at Elmley Castle

Font at Rock

In the parish churches of Worcestershire there survive thirteen engraved brasses, two incised slabs inlaid with pitch, about two dozen stone or alabaster effigies all originally set either on tomb chests or in niches, and a handful of pre-Reformation decorated coffin lids. Of the three dimensional effigies the knight of c1240 at Great Malvern is the earliest, and there are other 13th century knights at Tenbury Wells, Aston Somerville, Mamble and Pershore, plus a priest at Broadway. At Fladbury there are four brasses dating from 1445 to 1504, and three at Strensham, two of them high quality depictions of knights of 1390 and 1405. Kidderminster also has a fine brass of 1415 and other notable monuments of 1445 and c1490. Bredon has an early 14th century coffin lid with busts of a husband and wife set on either side of a cross. Martley, Bromsgrove and Stanford-on-Teme have fine 15th century alabaster effigies of knights on tomb chests. Generally these effigies represent the landed classes and there are few monuments to medieval tradesmen.

The Throckmorton brasses at Fladbury

Tomb of Sir Humphrey Salway, d1493 at Stanford-on-Teme

Daston Brass, Broadway

The double Sandys' tomb at Wickhamford.

Monuments of the period 1540-1700 are more common than those of the medieval period. Many of them continue the traditional medieval type tomb chest with recumbent effigies on top as at Bromsgrove, of c1550, where there are no Renaissance features yet introduced. Soon after then long back panels, columns, and top canopies start to appear. Particularly notable are the double monument of the 1630s to two generations at Wickhamford, the Savage monuments of the same decade at Inkberrow and Elmley Castle, the Russell monument at Strensham and the slightly earlier Berkeley monument at Spetchley. Besford has an alabaster effigy of the 1570s and a contemporary painted triptych with a kneeling figure of the deceased. Three dimensional kneeling figures occur in several places, and the early 17th century brasses at Stoke Prior also show kneeling figures. At Stockton-on-Teme is a rustic wooden canopied tomb without an effigy and at Mamble is a skeleton of c1561 instead of the usual clothed figure.

The emphasis on effigies decreased as the 17th century wore on. Eventually mural tablets with lengthy inscriptions became normal. Sometimes these have architectural surrounds, urns, cherubs, symbols of death or of a profession, and other adornments. During the 17th and 18th centuries there were made an ever increasing number of modest monuments to tradesmen and the middle classes generally.

GAZETTEER OF WORCESTERSHIRE CHURCHES

ABBERLEY   *St Michael*   SO 754678

A new church was built some distance to the NW in 1850-2 and the only part of the old church to remain roofed is the chancel, a Norman structure with an east end and side chapel of the 13th century. The walling of the nave and west tower, also Norman, is reduced to chest height, and the 13th century south aisle has lost its former three bay arcade. Reset in the aisle wall is the very worn original Norman south doorway. In the chancel is a monument of c1679 to members of the Walsh family.

ABBERTON   *St Eadburga*   SO 994535

A late Norman font decorated with bands of arrow-heads and chevrons lies in the present church of 1881-2 designed by W.J. Hopkins.

ABBOTS MORTON   *St Peter*   SO 027550

The church has a small main body with a blocked north doorway of c1200 and a north transept of the 14th century. The west tower is late 14th century. The chancel has ashlar faced east and south walls dated 1637. The rather delightful interior has old roofs, a plaster tympanum over the division between nave and chancel, and a Jacobean communion rail. The transept north window has 15th and 18th century glass and there are Flemish medallions dated 1590 in the east window of the chancel.

ALFRICK   *St Mary Magdalene*   SO 748529

The nave is Norman and retains three original windows and clasping pilaster buttresses at the west end. In the 13th century it was given a new south doorway, the east part of the north wall was rebuilt, and a larger new chancel was added. The chancel east window with reticulated tracery is 14th century and the porch and an adjacent window are of c1400. The north transept and vestry were added in 1895 by Aston Webb. A dado (with Victorian tracery) remains of the 15th century screen, and there are various round and oblong panels of 16th and 17th glass from the Netherlands. The font, the communion rail and a 12th century relief depicting a man have come from a former church (now in use as a house) at Lulsley.

Abberley Church

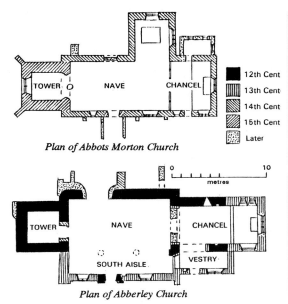

Plan of Abbots Morton Church

	12th Cent
	13th Cent
	14th Cent
	15th Cent
	Later

Plan of Abberley Church

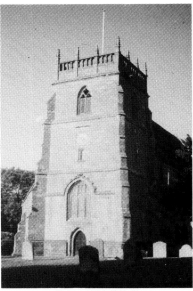

Tower, Alvechurch

ALVECHURCH   *St Laurence*   SP 026724

The Bishops of Worcester once had a house near this large church. A coffin lid with a foliated cross, chalice and shield commemorates Bishop Carpenter, d1476, and in the heavily restored 13th century chancel is the Bishops' chair with a wooden mitre above it. Except for the reset Norman south doorway, the whole of the south side is of 1859-61, when the church was rebuilt by Butterfield. Most of the wide north aisle and north chapel are 14th century work, but the blocked north doorway and an adjacent window are 15th century. The west tower is dated 1676, when it was rebuilt, but parts of it are older. A late 14th century cross-legged effigy of a knight lies in a niche in the north wall and there is a restored empty 15th century tomb recess in the chancel. There is a brass to Sir Philip Chatwyn, Gentleman Usher to Henry VIII, d1528, and a tablet and a cartouche in the Rococo style to Edward Moore, d1746.

Alfrick Church

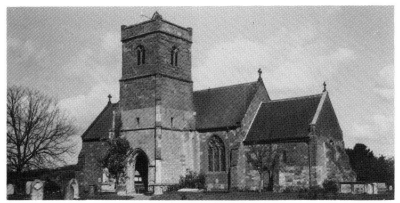

Areley Kings Church

ARELEY KINGS   *St Bartholomew*   SO 803710

The church was mostly rebuilt by Preedy in 1885-6 but the eastern part of the chancel is Norman with one original south window and an east window of c1800. The porch tower on the south side of the nave is 14th century with a 15th century upper half. The base of the font has an inscription which refers to Layamon, d1200, author of the chronicle known as Brut. The small figure with an hourglass came from a sundial of 1687.

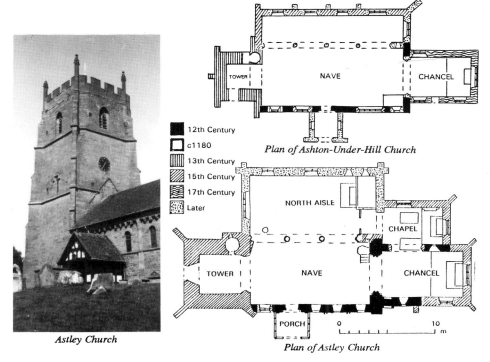

■ 12th Century
□ c1180
▥ 13th Century
▨ 15th Century
▧ 17th Century
▦ Later

Plan of Ashton-Under-Hill Church

Astley Church

Plan of Astley Church

ASHTON-UNDER-HILL   *St Barbara*   SO 997377

The most interesting part is the chancel with unusual tracery and fishes in the spandrels of the east window, and the date 1624 over the priest's doorway. The south doorway with a roll moulding in the arch indicates that the nave is Norman. The west tower and one south lancet are 13th century, the porch is probably 14th century, and the font, the south windows, and the heavily restored north aisle are all 15th century.

ASTLEY   *St Peter*   SO 787677

The nave and chancel of c1160 have unusually fine features. Below a string-course there are buttresses with two half shafts with a spur in between and above it the buttresses are semi-circular and have round headed windows between them. The south doorway is projected slightly forward and has two orders of columns and chevron ornamentation. The three bay north arcade was built in c1180. It now looks into an aisle which was rebuilt much wider than before in 1838. The west tower and north chapel are 15th century and the arch between the chapel and chancel is 16th century. The chancel east end is a Victorian rebuild. In the chapel are recumbent effigies of Walter Blount, d1561, and Robert Blount, d1573, and their wives. There are cartouches to Anne and Samuel Bowater, d1687 and 1696, and a white marble memorial with an urn in a recess to Thomas Winford, d1702. See photo on page 4.

ASTON SOMERVILLE   *Dedication Unknown*   SP 047379

The chancel has a priest's doorway of c1200 and windows of the 13th and 15th centuries. The nave may have a little Norman masonry and the much altered font may also have originally been Norman. The north doorway is 13th century. The nave windows are 14th century and probably of the same period as the former south transept of which only the blocked arch from the nave now remains. The tower was begun c1290-1300, perhaps sponsored by the knight whose mutilated chain mail clad effigy lies in the church. The screen is 15th century, the pulpit is partly Jacobean, and there is a monument to John and Rebecca Parry, d1714 and 1709.

Aston Somerville Church

BADSEY   *St James*   SP 071431

The Norman nave retains a blocked doorway on the north side. The Norman window west of it was in the south wall until 1885, when the south aisle and porch were added. The chancel and north transept are of the time of the dedication of 1295, but the chancel arch is Victorian. The hexagonal font is 14th century, and the west tower is 15th century. There are kneeling figures of Richard Hoby, d1617, and his wife and her children, and a tablet to William Jarret, d1685.

BAYTON   *St Bartholomew*   SO 691732

The wide Norman nave has a south doorway with chevron and lozenge patterns. The font is also Norman, having beaded scrolls and a rope moulding. The west tower is of 1817. The chancel has 15th century masonry, but its features, and the four nave windows, are all of 1905. A Jacobean pulpit lies inside the church.

BECKFORD   *St John The Baptist*   SO 976358

The spacious nave and the lower part of the central tower date from c1160-75. The nave has two Norman windows and traces of two others on either side of the large 15th century west window. The south doorway has two orders of columns and a tympanum with a cross, a roundel, a bird, and two animals, and the north doorway has a tympanum depicting the Harrowing of Hell, Christ being shown thrusting his cross into a dragon's mouth. The western tower arch is original but the east arch and middle stage of the tower are contemporary with the mid 13th century chancel. Transepts of c1200-50 were removed much later. A new top stage was added to the tower in the 18th century, making it very lofty. The chancel has a big Victorian vestry beside it. The font and several bench ends are 15th century, and there is a tablet to Richard Wakeman, d1662.

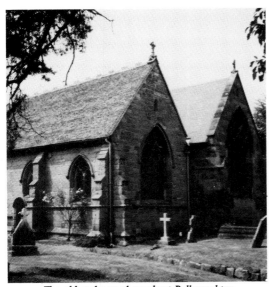

The old and new chancels at Belbroughton

Beckford Church

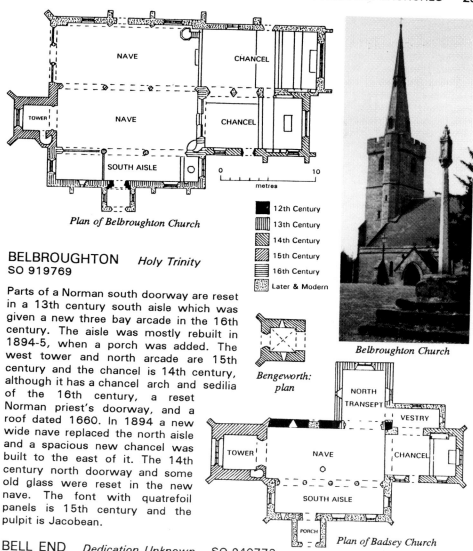

Plan of Belbroughton Church

12th Century
13th Century
14th Century
15th Century
16th Century
Later & Modern

Bengeworth: plan

Belbroughton Church

Plan of Badsey Church

BELBROUGHTON   *Holy Trinity*
SO 919769

Parts of a Norman south doorway are reset in a 13th century south aisle which was given a new three bay arcade in the 16th century. The aisle was mostly rebuilt in 1894-5, when a porch was added. The west tower and north arcade are 15th century and the chancel is 14th century, although it has a chancel arch and sedilia of the 16th century, a reset Norman priest's doorway, and a roof dated 1660. In 1894 a new wide nave replaced the north aisle and a spacious new chancel was built to the east of it. The 14th century north doorway and some old glass were reset in the new nave. The font with quatrefoil panels is 15th century and the pulpit is Jacobean.

BELL END   *Dedication Unknown*   SO 940772

In the garden of Bell Hall is a Norman chapel with original windows in the side walls and end wall mullioned windows and west buttresses of the 16th century.

BENGEWORTH   *Holy Trinity*   SP 045436

Only the lowest stage of the 14th century west tower now survives of the old church. It once had a spire. The chancel was also 14th century and was flanked by 15th century north and south chapels. Monuments to Thomas Watson, d1561, and John Deacle, d1709, have been transferred to the new church of 1870-2 by T.D. Barry.

BEOLEY   *St Leonard*   SP 065697

The unmoulded early 12th century chancel arch lies on plain imposts. In c1230-50 the chancel was lengthened and the nave was given a north chapel and a narrow south aisle with a three bay arcade. In c1300 the chapel became the eastern part of a north aisle with a three bay north arcade. In c1400 the west tower with diagonal buttresses was added, the south aisle mostly rebuilt, and new windows inserted in the north aisle and chancel. Ralph Sheldon built a wide chapel on the north side of the chapel in the 1580s. In round arches between the chancel and chapel are tombs with effigies of William Sheldon, d1570, and Ralph himself, d1613, and their wives. In the chapel are two more tomb chests and many other memorials to the family, plus a 13th century coffin lid with a foliated cross. The church also has some fragments of old glass, a 12th century relief of an abbot in mass vestments, and a font with female heads.

BERROW   *St Faith*   SO 794344

The nave north wall and north doorway are Norman and there is a 13th century north lancet. The chancel is 14th century but with a 15th century east window. The west tower is late 14th century, and the narrow south aisle and three bay arcade are 15th century. The font with rope patterns is Norman, and the pulpit is 17th century.

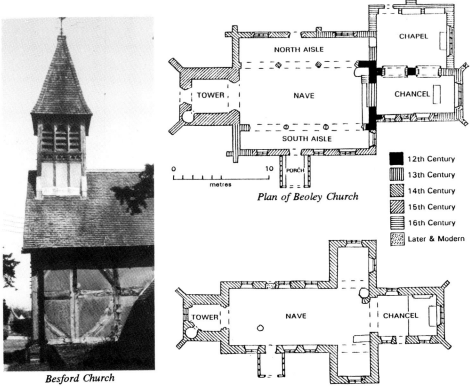

Besford Church

Plan of Beoley Church

- ■ 12th Century
- ▦ 13th Century
- ▨ 14th Century
- ▧ 15th Century
- ▤ 16th Century
- ▦ Later & Modern

Plan of Birtsmorton Church

Bewdley Church

Tomb of Admiral William Caldwall, Birtsmorton

BESFORD   *St Peter*   SO 911448

The rare timber framed nave dates from the 14th century and has posts carrying the tie-beams upon which are queen-posts. The rood loft parapet and part of the original screen also survive, but the church as a whole was heavily restored by Hopkins in 1880-1, when the stone chancel and vestry, the nave plinth, and the belfry were added. Inside are panelling and a communion rail of the 17th century, a recumbent alabaster effigy of Richard Harewell, d1576 aged 15, a late 16th century painted tryptich to another Harewell, and a monument to Sir Edward Sebright, d1679.

BEWDLEY   *St Anne*   SO 786753

A timber framed 15th century chapel-of-ease to Ribbesford once lay on this cramped and sloping site forming an island without a burial ground in the middle of the main street of the town. It was given a lofty west tower in 1695-6, to which Thomas Woodward of Chipping Campden in 1745-8 added a new Classical style church with Tuscan columns, a plaster tunnel vault and a Venetian east window. The pulpit is also mid 18th century.

BIRLINGHAM   *St James*   SO 932431

The church was entirely rebuilt in 1871-2 by Benjamin Ferry except for the 15th century tower projecting westwards beyond the south aisle.

BIRTSMORTON   *St Peter and St Paul*   SO 801355

The nave, small transepts and chancel are all 14th century. Despite many of the windows having been renewed, numerous fragments of 14th and 15th century glass have survived. The west tower is 15th century. There is a mid 18th century communion table and a piece of embroidery with the Hastings arms and the date 1693. The tomb chest of c1500 with the damaged indent of a brass and the figures of husbands and children around the sides is likely to be that of Jane Nanfan. There is also a tablet to Bridges Nanfan, d1704, and a semi-reclining effigy and warship to Admiral William Caldwall, d1718. See front cover picture.

BISHAMPTON   *St Peter*   SO 990519

In 1870-1 Preedy rebuilt the church except for the big 15th century west tower with diagonal buttresses and corner pinnacles. He reused the Norman south and north doorways and one round headed window. He also retained the Norman font with crosses, rosettes, and a rope moulding, and the pulpit hourglass stand.

BOCKLETON   *St Michael*   SO 593614

The fine nave of c1160-70 has pilaster buttresses, four original windows and splendid north and south doorways with one order of columns, rolls in the arches, crenellation and lozenge chains, and blind arcades of interlaced arches. In the late 13th century a larger new chancel was built and new windows inserted in the eastern bay of the nave. The north chapel may be medieval but now has 19th century windows and a two bay arcade. The tower arch is of c1200 but the existing tower is probably 18th century. The 16th century recess in the nave NE corner was made to contain a tomb chest which has been removed. In the chapel are recumbent sandstone effigies of the 1590s of Richard Barneby and his wife, and a monument to Charles Baldwin, d1706.

BRANSFORD   *St John The Baptist*   SO 797516

The earliest feature of the single chamber with a fine wagon roof is a 13th century lancet on the south side. The south doorway and adjacent window are 14th century and much of the rest is 15th century. A 17th century timber framed wall divides off the west end where there are posts for a bell turret. One north window contains some glass of c1400 and there is a Jacobean communion rail. Mural paintings discovered in 1957 have now mostly been recovered.

BREDICOT   *St James*   SO 905550

This is a small single bodied late 13th century church which was heavily restored in 1843. There are 15th century tiles in the porch.

Bockleton Church

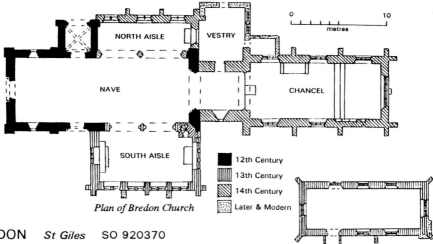

Plan of Bredon Church

North Aisle

Vestry

Nave

Chancel

South Aisle

- ■ 12th Century
- ▥ 13th Century
- ▨ 14th Century
- ▦ Later & Modern

Plan of Bredicot Church

BREDON   *St Giles*   SO 920370

This is an interesting church with an unusual layout. The Norman nave has clasping pilaster buttresses on the west corners, an original window at the west end of each of the north and south walls, a plain corbel table, and three original doorways each with one order of columns. The rib-vaulted north porch is also Norman, a rare example of such an early porch in a parish church. In the mid 13th century a wide south chapel with two light windows with trefoiled heads and a two bay arcade was added east of the south doorway. The splendid chancel arch of c1190 now looks into the lowest stage of a central tower of c1300-10 with a spacious three bay chancel of the same date beyond it. The chancel has three light side windows, a four light east window, and there are sedilia and a piscina on the south side. The narrow north aisle with a two bay arcade was added c1330-50, and the rood stair and the large west window are 15th century. Only the vestry on the north side of the tower is modern. See p14.

In the chancel are 14th century tiles bearing the arms of 38 different families, plus those of a former rector who later became Bishop Trelleck of Hereford. Also of the 14th century are the Easter Sepulchre recess with ballflower ornamentation and a cross-slab, some old glass, and the fine coffin lid with a cross and canopied busts of a man and woman. There is also a recess of c1500 with three effigies of that period. In the south aisle is a splendid alabaster monument with effigies of Giles Reed, d1611, and his wife, and a heart and hands of c1290 commemorating a heart burial.

Bredon Church

BREDON'S NORTON   *St Giles*   SO 931390

Much of this long unaisled church dates from Preedy's restoration of 1883 but the nave has an original lancet in each of the north and west walls, the latter now looking into a 13th century tower. The chancel arch is also 13th century and the south doorway has reset fragments of c1175-90 with chevrons and other motifs. A tablet to William Hancocke, d1719, and his wife, d1685, was made while he was still alive.

BRETFORTON   *St Leonard*   SP 093438

The eastern two arches of the south arcade are of c1190 and the three bay north arcade with scallops and heads (plus the legend of St Margaret) on the capitals is of c1200-10. In the late 13th century and early 14th century the aisles were rebuilt, the eastern part of each being widened into a small transept. The western arch of the south side was made in the 15th century when the west tower was added. The spacious chancel with cusped lancet windows was consecrated in 1295, and the north and south porches are Victorian. There is some 17th century woodwork in the south transept and there are fragments of old glass in the north aisle windows. See p6.

BRICKLEHAMPTON   *St Michael*   SO 982424

Most of the church was rebuilt in 1876 but the nave masonry and the south doorway with one order of columns and chevrons is 12th century and one south window is late 13th century. The Norman font has on it two crosses and two rosettes.

BROADWAS   *St Mary Magdalene*   SO 755552

The long nave and chancel are mostly of c1200, the south doorway and several windows being of that period. The west end with triple lancets is later. The two bay south chapel with a quatrefoil shaped pier in the arcade must be of about the period of a chantry being founded here in 1344. West of it is the old timber framed porch. The space below the timber bell turret is divided off by a timber partition and has a Jacobean balcony railing. There is a monument inside to Henry Roberts, d1761.

Broadway Church

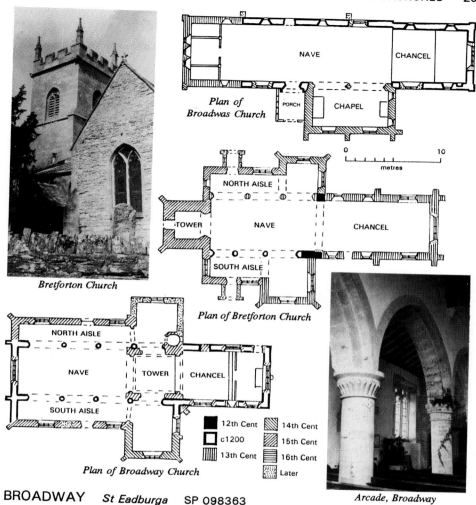

Plan of
Broadwas Church

NAVE

CHANCEL

PORCH

CHAPEL

0   10
metres

NORTH AISLE

TOWER   NAVE   CHANCEL

SOUTH AISLE

Bretforton Church

Plan of Bretforton Church

NORTH AISLE

NAVE   TOWER   CHANCEL

SOUTH AISLE

■ 12th Cent   ⬚ 14th Cent
☐ c1200   ▨ 15th Cent
▥ 13th Cent   ▤ 16th Cent
▦ Later

Plan of Broadway Church

Arcade, Broadway

BROADWAY   *St Eadburga*   SP 098363

The church lies far from the village down a back lane. Although it is cruciform it is not particularly large. By the 1190s it consisted of a nave with narrow aisles and four bay arcades and a chancel of the same width. New lancet windows, now blocked, were inserted in the chancel in the 13th century and c1300 the east bays of the nave were widened out into transepts. About a century later a crossing was created in the east bay of the nave with a tower above it, and the aisles were rebuilt without being widened. The chancel NE doorway and the south transept east window are insertions of c1600 and the north transept was rebuilt in 1866. The pulpit, screen, and chancel benches incorporate medieval woodwork, and there are 15th century tiles by the font. There are also fragments of old glass, and a 17th century communion rail. In the south transept are pieces of a late 13th century effigy of a priest. The brass to Anthony Daston, d1572, in the chancel is engraved on the reverse of an older Flemish brass. There are tablets to Walter Savage, d1641, and William Taylor, d1741.

BROMSGROVE   *St John The Baptist*   SO 956706

This large church lies on a hill above the town. Some Norman masonry remains at all four corners of the nave, those at the west end have pilasters towards the north and south. By the end of the 13th century the church had almost attained its present size, having been given a new chancel and spacious aisles. A tower with bold diagonal buttresses was then begun but the arch and the upper parts with a spire are 15th century, whilst the west doorway looks like 13th century work reset. Also 15th century are the four bay south arcade, the south porch, the aisle windows, the embattled clerestory, the eastern part of the north aisle, and the chapel extending east to the west wall of the 13th century north vestry. The east arch of the north arcade and the outer vestry with a north facing polygonal bay are modern.

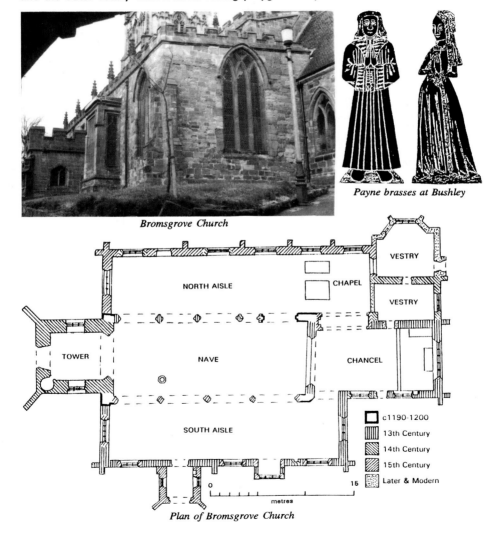

Payne brasses at Bushley

Bromsgrove Church

Plan of Bromsgrove Church

The monuments at Bromsgrove make up for the lack of old furnishings. On tomb chests in the north chapel are alabaster effigies of Humphrey Stafford, d1450, and Sir John Talbot, d1501, and their wives. In the chancel is an alabaster effigy of Lady Talbot of Grafton Manor, d1517, and a tablet to Bishop Hall of Bristol, d1710. In the south aisle is the semi-reclining figure of George Lytelton, d1600. Two defaced effigies and a coffin lid with a foliated cross lie in a bay window tomb recess.

BROOME   *St Peter*   SO 902784

This small brick 18th century church has a pyramidal roofed west tower containing the entrance, an east end of 1861, and a crudely ornamented Norman font.

BROUGHTON HACKETT   *St Leonard*   SO 924546

The nave is probably 12th century and the chancel perhaps 13th century, but the 14th century west window is the earliest datable feature of the single chamber. The south wall and most of the features are Victorian.

BUSHLEY   *St Peter*   SO 875344

The church was rebuilt in 1843 and given a new chancel in 1856. It contains brasses of Thomas Payne, d1500, and his wife, plus several 17th and 18th century monuments to the Dowdeswells of Pull Court. In the grounds of their house is a folly of 1843 incorporating two 14th century windows from the original church.

CASTLEMORTON   *St Gregory*   SO 795373

The Norman nave and chancel have several original windows and the north doorway and reset south doorway both have chevrons. The four bay south arcade and the south aisle appear to have been added in the 13th century and the south transept seems to have replaced the aisle east bay c1300, but there has been rebuilding some time after 1647, when the church was reported as being in a decayed state. The west tower, several windows and the timber north porch are 15th century. The communion rail is dated 1683 and 1684. There is a broken 15th century font and also an 18th century font. A chancel south window contains fragments of old glass.

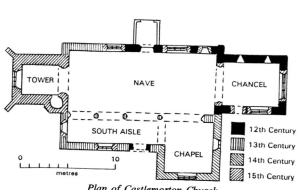

Plan of Castlemorton Church

Castlemorton Church

Font at Chaddesley Corbett

Chaddesley Corbett Church

CHADDESLEY CORBETT

St Cassian   SO 891735

This is a particularly interesting and impressive church. The three eastern bays of the north arcade are mid 12th century. The wider western arch and the three arches on the south side are of c1190 but have been re-assembled later to lengthen the nave as far as an added west tower. The tower arch looks 14th century but a new 18th century tower with its own narrower arch has been built against it in place of the medieval tower. The south aisle was rebuilt in the 14th century and given new windows in the 16th century. The north aisle was rebuilt in the 19th century except for the Norman north doorway. The finest part of the church is the 14th century chancel with intersecting tracery forms in the south and east windows. North of it is a 16th century vestry set east of a three bay chapel of c1280 with a two bay arcade.

Of c1160-70 is the very fine font decorated with bands of interlace and four dragons. There is a late 13th century limestone cross-legged effigy of a knight. The effigy of a priest is probably 15th century. There are also worn brasses of Thomas Forest, d1511 and his family, and a fine monument to Humfrey Packington, d1631. In the north chapel is a monument of alabaster and marble to Elizabeth Holt, d1647.

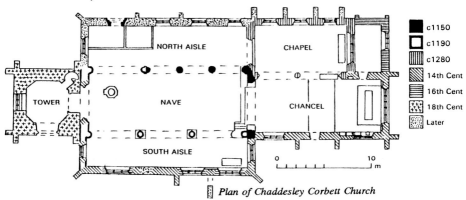

Plan of Chaddesley Corbett Church

CHILDSWICKHAM   *St Mary*   SP 075385

The nave south and north walls are Victorian but there is a fine west doorway of c1130-40 with one order of columns and a contemporary window above. Both now look into a 14th century tower with a later top having a recessed spire. A second Norman window is reset in the 13th century north transept which has a two light window with plate tracery in the north wall. The chancel was intended to be vaulted in two bays and is also 13th century. On the north side is the blocked arch of a destroyed small 15th century chapel. The font with elementary patterns on it is probably of the 1660s.

CHURCH HONEYBOURNE   *St Ecwin*   SP 144436

A dedication is recorded in 1295 and the leaning tower, nave, and chancel are all of about that time. There was also in that period a south aisle with a four bay arcade. It was demolished in the 14th century and only two blocked arcade arches remain of it. The south porch with a stone roof on transverse arches and the clerestory on the south side and the nave roof are 15th century. The spire is of the 1360s. The tower has a big later NW buttress and a Victorian south doorway. See plan on page 7.

CHURCHILL   *St Michael*   SO 923536

Most of the features of the nave and chancel date from the heavy restoration of 1910 but the south doorway and chancel arch are 13th or 14th century. The panelling, the communion rail and the pulpit may all be 17th century and there is a shield of old glass with the Wisham arms in the east window. There is a cartouche to Thomas Barker, d1688, and there are two fragments of a figure of a lion from another monument.

Church Honeybourne Church

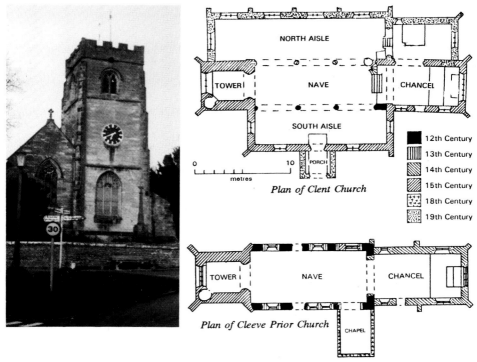

NORTH AISLE

TOWER   NAVE   CHANCEL

SOUTH AISLE

0   10   PORCH
  metres

Plan of Clent Church

■ 12th Century
▥ 13th Century
▧ 14th Century
▨ 15th Century
▦ 18th Century
▩ 19th Century

TOWER   NAVE   CHANCEL

Plan of Cleeve Prior Church   CHAPEL

CHURCH LENCH   *All Saints*   SO 024513

The nave north wall with its doorway and the reset south doorway are late 12th century. The two western bays of the aisle are 14th century and so probably was the now much renewed chancel. Of the 15th century are the west tower, the rood stair, several windows including the clerestory, the trussed rafter roof over the chancel, and the eastern part of the aisle which probably replaces a former south transept. There is an early 16th century cope of blue velvet with the orphreys with saints being split vertically for re-use as a border.

CLEEVE PRIOR   *St Andrew*   SO 088494

The nave has a Norman north doorway but is otherwise mostly 13th century There are transept arches of c1210, that on the north being blocked and that one the south now opening into an 18th century chapel with Victorian windows. The late 13th century chancel was heavily restored in 1863. The west tower is 15th century.

CLENT   *St Leonard*   SO 928794

The three bay south arcade is late 12th century. The aisle itself the west tower, and the chancel inclined to the south, and the wagon roof are all 15th century. On the south doorway is the inscription "Jaxta hunc lapidem jacet corpus Johnannis Cleye". In 1864-5 Kirke and Parry added the south porch, the north vestry, and replaced a north aisle of 1837 by another embracing the tower. Amongst several tablets is one of c1650 in the Baroque style with twisted columns and an open segmental pediment.

CLIFTON-UPON-TEME   *St Kenelm*   SO 715615

The nave, chancel, and west tower with several lancet windows, are all 13th century. The south aisle with its three bay arcade were added c1320, perhaps at the expense of the knight whose cross-legged effigy remains. In the aisle east window are fragments of old glass. There are tablets by Grinling Gibbons to Henry Jefferys and Lady Winnington, d1688 and 1718. See photo page 10.

COFTON HACKET

St Michael   SP 012754

Much of the church was rebuilt in 1861 by Henry Day, but the chancel masonry is 14th century and also medieval are the western buttresses, the pinnacled double bellcote and the timber porch. Inside are many 17th and 18th century tablets to the Joliffes and an incised slab to William Leycester, d1508.

Plan of Clifton-upon-Teme Church

■ 12th Century
▥ 13th Century
▨ 14th Century
▧ 15th Century
▩ 17th Century
▦ Later & Modern

COTHERIDGE

St Leonard   SO 785547

The church is whitewashed all over except for the upper parts of the very unusual timber framed porch tower of c1300 on the south side. The wide nave and chancel with pilaster buttresses are both Norman. They are connected by a very narrow arch flanked by 15th century arches of the same width. The nave has a 15th century south window and others of the 18th or 19th century. The chancel has 14th century south windows. The north chapel was added in 1620. The pulpit and tester are mid 17th century, the communion rail is 18th century, and the chancel floor tiles are 15th century.

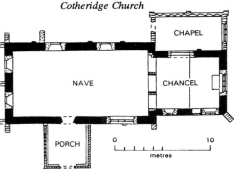

Cotheridge Church

Cleeve Prior Church

Plan of Cotheridge Church

COW HONEYBOURNE   *Dedication Unknown*   SP 120440

The church was rebuilt in 1861-3 by Hopkins except for the 15th century west tower. The church is now used as a house.

CROOME D'ABITOT   *St Mary Magdalene*   SO 887850

The Coventry family had this church built on a virgin site in 1763. It is likely that it was designed by Capability Brown, but with an interior and furnishings by Robert Adam. Although originally intended to be in the Classical style, the church is in fact Gothic with cusped intersecting tracery, a high vaulted porch under the west tower, and slender piers carrying a plaster tunnel vault over the nave. The chancel is unusually long for its period and is filled with splendid monuments brought in from the long-destroyed old church. They are of Thomas, 1st Lord Coventry, d1639, the 2nd Lord Coventry, d1661, and his wife, Sir Henry Coventry, d1686, and the 4th Lord Coventry, d1687, the last being designed by Grinling Gibbons. See photo on p10.

Tombs at Croome D'Abitot

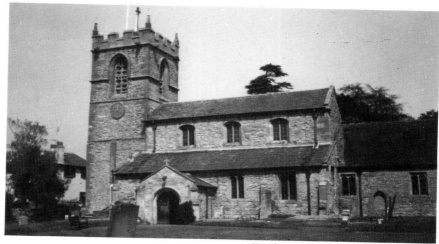

Cropthorne Church

CROPTHORNE   *St Michael*   SO 001452

The four bay north and south arcades with plain round arches are of c1120 and c1150 respectively, whilst the lower part of the tower with mid wall pilaster buttresses pierced by small windows is of c1180. A new chancel and chancel arch were built in c1200-20. The chancel was lengthened and the aisles widened in the 14th century. The chancel was again rebuilt using the old materials in 1894. Of the late 15th century are the south porch, originally of two storeys, and the tower top. The coffin lid of a priest lies in an ogival headed recess in the north aisle. There are recumbent effigies of Francis Dinely, d1624, and his wife and under the north arcade east bay are kneeling figures of Edward Dinely, d1646, and his wife. See plan on page 7.

CROWLE   *St John The Baptist*   SO 922559

The rebuilding of 1881-5 by Preedy left only the early 16th century tower arch, the 14th century timber porch with an original roof, the 15th century font, and a lectern, which, although much restored, has a fine carving of c1200 of a kneeling man on it.

DEFFORD   *St James*   SO 917432

The Norman nave has south windows of c1600 and north windows of the time of the Victorian chancel. Over the segmental headed south doorway is a fine female head used as the keystone. The west tower dates from the 15th century and has a timber framed upper stage. The west gallery is late Georgian.

Defford Church

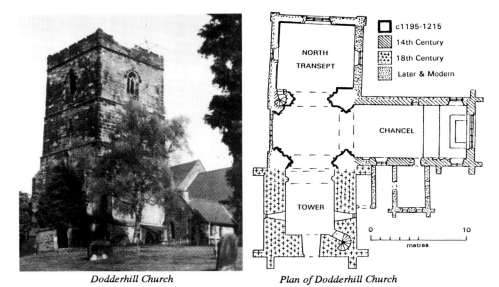

Dodderhill Church

Plan of Dodderhill Church

DODDERHILL   *St Augustine*   SO 902637

This interesting church lies on a hill overlooking Droitwich. As begun in the 1190s, and consecrated in 1220, it was cruciform with a central tower. From it there remain the four crossing arches. A new chancel with ogival headed sedilia and piscina was built in the early 14th century. The upper part of the crossing tower was taken down after the Civil War and in 1708 a large and massive new tower incorporating some older material was built on the site of the old south transept. By the early 19th century the nave had been taken down, the western crossing arch blocked, and the north transept and the chancel north wall mostly rebuilt. Inside is part of a monument of c1620 with four kneeling children to one of the Dannet family.

St Peter's Church, Droitwich

DORMSTON   *St Nicholas*   SO 987576

The small nave, the mostly rebuilt chancel and the timber framed south porch were all built in the 14th century. The timber framed west tower with heavy bracing inside was added in the 15th century. The crucifixion relief is probably from the head of a former cross out in the churchyard. See photo on page 10.

DOVERDALE   *St Mary*   SO 860660

Much of the church dates from Preedy's restoration of 1860 but the nave has two 17th century windows and panelling and the masonry may be yet older. In one north window is a 15th century stained glass figure of the Virgin Mary.

DROITWICH   *St Andrew*   SO 900634

The chancel arch and the north transeptal tower with arches to the west. east and south are early 13th century. The arches have many heads on the crocketted capitals. The church was mostly rebuilt after a fire in the late 13th century and the nave west wall, the three bay arcades, the south aisle and the south chapel with its two bay arcade are all early 14th century work, whilst the north chapel dates from the end of that century. The chancel east wall was rebuilt in 1928 and the north aisle in c1910. There are fragments of old glass in the south chapel. The font is probably Jacobean. There is a tablet to Coningby Norbury, d1734.

DROITWICH   *St Peter*   SO 903624

The church lies on a hill SE of the town. The Norman chancel has three small north windows and a shafted chancel arch. A south aisle and south transept were added to the nave in the 13th century, but the aisle was later removed, leaving only its blocked arcade. There are two arches in the transept west wall so either the aisle was remarkably wide or the transept itself had an unusual western aisle or chapel. The north transept is 14th century and the west tower is 15th century. The nave north wall is 16th century but contains a 14th century window. The timber framed clerestory is probably 16th century and the font is Jacobean. There are 15th century tiles by the font and in the Victorian north vestry and the south transept has some 14th century glass. There is an effigy of George Wylde, Serjeant-at-Law, d1616, and a tablet to Richard Nash, d1690.

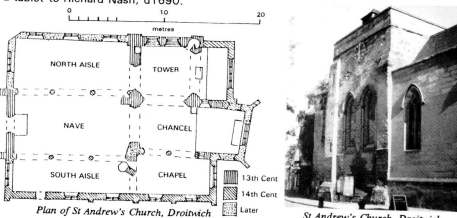

Plan of St Andrew's Church, Droitwich   *St Andrew's Church, Droitwich*

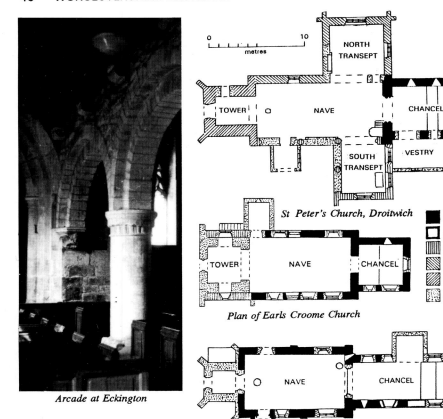

St Peter's Church, Droitwich

■	12th Cent
□	c1200
▥	13th Cent
▨	14th Cent
▨	15th Cent
▦	Later

Plan of Earls Croome Church

Arcade at Eckington

Plan of Eastham Church

EARLS CROOME   *St Nicholas*   SO 870420

The nave and chancel are both Norman with several original window embrasures, two
of which in the chancel have 13th century outer openings. The narrow chancel arch
has one leaf capital with entwined trails and there are blocked Norman doorways in
the nave. In the 1840s a neo-Norman tower was set into the western part of the nave,
a vestry added, and several of the windows renewed.

EASTHAM   *St Peter and St Paul*   SO 657688

The nave and chancel of tufa blocks with pilaster buttresses and a south doorway set
in a projection with intersecting blank arches above are both Norman. At the end of
the 12th century the chancel was doubled in length and shortly afterwards a new
north doorway with a continuous keeled roll was inserted in the nave. Three windows
are late 13th century, and the brick west tower is of 1825. High up on either side of
the Victorian chancel arch are Norman sculptured panels and there are two more
outside. The cauldron shaped font with a rope moulding at its foot is also Norman. The
pulpit and the chancel walls have 17th century panels and the chancel has a roundel
of c1535 in a window recess on the south side.

ECKINGTON   *Holy Trinity*   SO 922413

The western part of the nave and the three bay south arcade are of c1190-1200. The west doorway has side shafts with stiff-leaf capitals and an arch with crenellations and lozenges set round an angle. The aisle has a late 13th century east window and a Victorian outer facing. A probable fourth bay has been replaced by a 15th century tower. The 14th century chancel contains a monument with kneeling effigies of John Hanford, d1616, and his wife. The wide north aisle is of 1830 but the arcade and vestries at each end are of 1887.

ELDERSFIELD   *St John The Baptist*   SO 799312

The chancel with a much restored chancel arch and parts of the nave walls are Norman. Traces of a Norman doorway can be seen by the present doorway on the south side. The chancel has 13th and 14th century windows and the north aisle and its four bay arcade are 14th century. The south transept, the recut font, and the west tower with a recessed spire are 15th century. The pulpit is Jacobean but contains pieces from a medieval screen. The benches with linenfold panels are 16th century. There are several 17th century coats-of-arms in stained glass, one being dated 1629.

ELMBRIDGE   *St Mary*   SO 899678

The church was rebuilt in 1872 except for the three bay north arcade and the south doorway with two orders of columns, both of c1190-1200. There is tablet to Edmund Pershall, d1650.

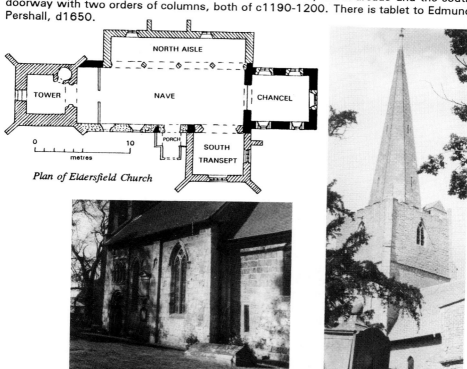

Plan of Eldersfield Church

Eastham Church

Eldersfield Church

Savage tomb, Elmley Castle Church

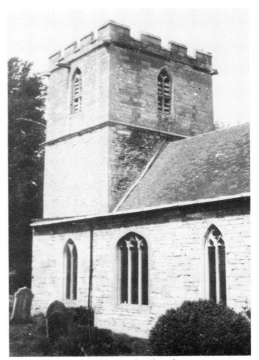

Elmley Castle Church

ELMLEY CASTLE   *St Mary*   SO 982410

This is one of the most interesting churches in Worcestershire. The chancel has herringbone masonry and is probably as old as the 11th century. With it went a nave corresponding to the present one, although openings made for later additions have obliterated the walls of that period. The low west tower and the base of the font are 13th century. The 14th century south aisle has a four bay arcade which appears to have been built in two campaigns because the two western bays have solid chunks of wall instead of pillars. However these latter parts may be connected with the rebuilding recorded by a date stone of 1629 on the wall outside. Except for the slightly earlier east bay of the arcade and a probably 13th century arch reset in the porch outer entrance, the north aisle, porch, and transept are all late medieval. They form an embattled show front facing the village. The small stones with a rabbit and a pig in the porch and various architectural fragments reset in the walls are Norman. The south aisle east window has some fragments of old glass. In the transept are the splendid recumbent effigies of William and Giles Savage, d1631, and the latter's wife. There is also a foliated medieval coffin lid and a very fine monument by William Stanton to the 1st Earl of Coventry, d1699. See photo on page 4 and drawing on page 15.

ELMLEY LOVETT   *St Michael*   SO 866697

Only the 14th century west tower with a recessed spire with roll mouldings up the angles and a 17th century oak chest survived the rebuilding of 1839-40.

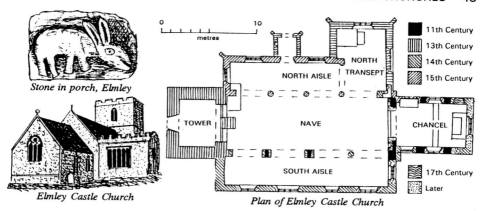

Stone in porch, Elmley

Elmley Castle Church

Plan of Elmley Castle Church

■ 11th Century
▥ 13th Century
▨ 14th Century
▧ 15th Century

▤ 17th Century
▦ Later

EVESHAM   *All Saints*   SP 037437

There are two medieval churches set side by side in the precinct of the destroyed abbey church. All Saints served as the parish church. Most of it, comprising a small west tower with a west porch, the wide aisles with three bay arcades, and the large transepts are 15th century. On the south side is a small but fine fan-vaulted chapel built by Abbot Lichfield in c1510-13 when he was still only the Prior. The nave west doorway is of c1200 and the arches to the north transept and chancel, plus one south window, are 14th century, whilst the chancel is Victorian. Inside are a 15th century font, several bosses and a late 13th or 14th century seated figure of Moses from the Abbey church, and a monument to Elizabeth Baylies, d1754. One north window contains 14th century glass showing Christ seated. See photo on page 8.

All Saints' Church, Evesham

Interior of Fladbury Church

St Lawrence, Evesham

Plan of St Lawrence's Church, Evesham

NORTH AISLE

TOWER

NAVE

CHANCEL

SOUTH AISLE

CHAPEL

▨ 15th Century

▤ 16th Century

▨ Later & Modern

EVESHAM   *St Lawrence*   SP 036436

This church served the parochial cemetery.

It was entirely rebuilt in the 15th century with wide aisles and arcades of four and three bays respectively to the narrow nave and chancel, with a length of walling on each side between marking the site of the rood screen. The nave is quite narrow and undoubtedly represents the size of the original modest chapel dedicated in 1295. A fan vaulted chapel was added on the south side in the early 16th century. The north aisle was destroyed in 1730 and the church lay in a ruinous state until a new aisle and arcade plus a new spire on the tower were built in 1836 by H. Eginton.

FECKENHAM   *St John The Baptist*   SP 009616

The NE corner of the Norman nave survives, and the 15th century north aisle has a reset doorway of c1200. The wind-blown stiff-leaf capital of one of the pillars of the four bay arcade dates it to c1240-50. The substantial west tower is 15th century. In 1853 Butterfield rebuilt the chancel, probably with facsimiles of the 12th and 13th century windows of the original, and the nave south wall was rebuilt and given a porch by Day of Worcester in 1866-7. The inscription to Sir Martin Culpepper, d1604, was formerly upon a tomb which was removed in 1853.

FLADBURY   *St John The Baptist*   SO 996463

The Norman lower part of the tower has pilaster buttresses at the corners and in the middle of the sides, the latter being pierced by windows. In the latter part of the 13th century the walls were thickened internally and heightened. The four bay arcades and the aisles and the rib vaulted porch (which originally had an upper floor) are mid to late 14th century. The chancel was mostly rebuilt in the 1860s by Preedy, but there are 14th century stained glass shields in a north window, and a Virgin and Child in a vestry window. Under the tower is a large tomb chest with fine brasses of John Throckmorton, d1445 and his wife, and there is a brass half figure of the priest Thomas Morden, d1458, plus other brasses to Edward Peytoo, d1488, and William Plewme, d1504, in the chancel. There is a standing monument (which has been re-arranged) to Bishop Lloyd, d1717, and the best of several tablets is that to Elizabeth Charlet, d1746. See p16.

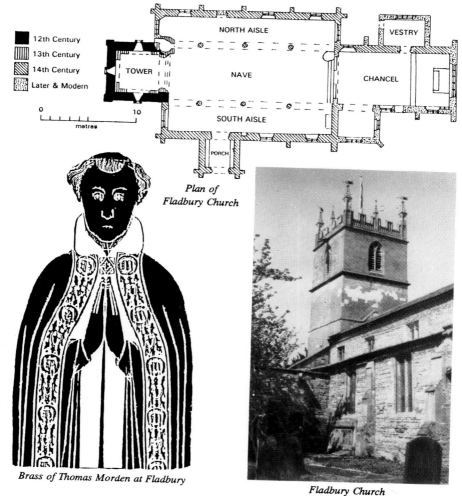

12th Century
13th Century
14th Century
Later & Modern

0   metres   10

NORTH AISLE

VESTRY

TOWER

NAVE

CHANCEL

SOUTH AISLE

PORCH

Plan of Fladbury Church

Brass of Thomas Morden at Fladbury

Fladbury Church

FLYFORD FLAVELL   *St Peter*   SO 979550

The nave, chancel, and north transept are mostly of 1883 by Hopkins but with some old materials. The west tower is probably mostly 15th century. Below it are some contemporary tiles. Fragments of old stained glass lie in a south window.

FRANKLEY   *St Leonard*   SO 999804

The church looks out over reservoirs and high tower blocks among Birmingham suburbia. The nave west wall may be Norman and the west of the walling is late medieval or 17th century. The windows, the porch, and the chancel and vestry are all Georgian or Victorian. The short tower built inside the nave in 1751 has new tripartitite supports provided in 1931 after a fire which destroyed the old roofs. In the churchyard is a very worn Saxon cross-shaft with interlace and traces of scrolls.

GRAFTON FLYFORD   *St John The Baptist*   SO 963557

The church was mostly rebuilt in 1875 but retains some windows and a west tower with a dwarf recessed spire of the 14th century, some fragments of old glass in the east and west windows, a 15th century pulpit, 16th century painted signs of St John and St Mark on square boards, and a tablet to Roger Stonehall, d1645.

GRAFTON MANOR   *St Michael*   SO 939691

Beside the house (which is now a country house hotel), and connected with it, is a 15th century chapel comprising a nave, chancel, and bellcote. The west gallery is of c1800, i.e just after the chapel was restored from a ruinous state. The chapel contained monuments to the Talbots, once lords of the manor.

GREAT COMBERTON   *St Michael*   SO 954420

The west tower has side chambers making it the same width as the thick-walled nave which is probably Norman. The tower and chambers are 15th century but the three arches under the tower look Early Norman and could be a relic of a former crossing tower with what is now the nave as its chancel. The windows of the present chancel and nave are 14th century, and the chancel arch, vestries, and east window are Victorian. The stalls have 17th century panels, and there are 16th century benches.

GREAT MALVERN   *St Mary and St Michael*   SO 776459

This church perched on a sloping site on the east side of the Malvern Hills originally served a Benedictine priory founded in 1085. The arcades of six bays of double-stepped round arches on short but thick round piers are relics of a new church built c1120. Between 1420 and 1460 the exterior of the building was entirely rebuilt. Such a complete rebuilding of a monastic church in this period is a rarity in England, and the work is of the highest order with much panelling in the facades and battlements and over the whole of the upper part of the central tower. There are west and east windows of exceptional size with nine and eight lights respectively. The aisles have vaults but an intended vault in the chancel was never erected. Below the east window there was once a Lady Chapel removed in the 16th century when the rest of the church was saved from destruction by being taken over by the town. The presence of a cloister prevented the south aisle from being widened. On that side are a Norman doorway and windows of 1841. The church was decayed in 1833 but was restored 1860-1, and the two storey north porch rebuilt in 1894. See photo on page 10.

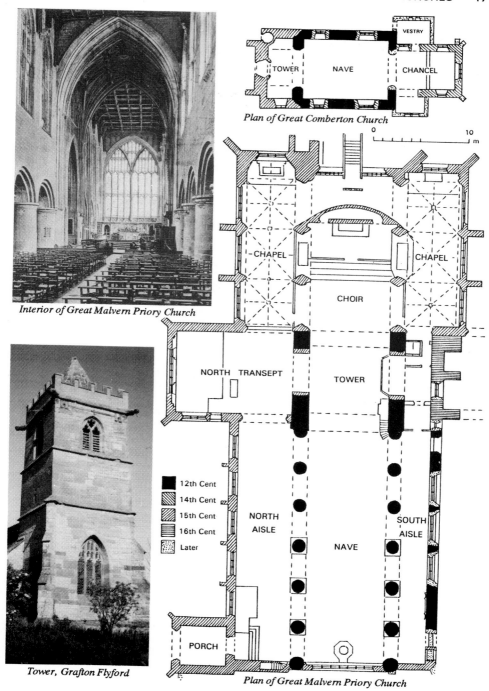

Plan of Great Comberton Church

Interior of Great Malvern Priory Church

Tower, Grafton Flyford

Plan of Great Malvern Priory Church

TOWER NAVE CHANCEL VESTRY

0 10 m

CHAPEL CHAPEL

CHOIR

NORTH TRANSEPT TOWER

12th Cent
14th Cent
15th Cent
16th Cent
Later

NORTH AISLE

SOUTH AISLE

NAVE

PORCH

Great Malvern Priory Church

The stained glass windows at Great Malvern dating from c1440-1506 are the most complete set of their period in Britain. Old Testament stories appear in the south chapel, the east window has scenes from the Passion and the apostles, the chancel clerestory includes the stories of the Virgin and St Werstan, and the north transept end windows has figures of Henry VII (who donated the window c1502), and his Queen and Prince Arthur. The west window originally contained the Last Judgement and the Virgin and six Virgin martyrs, but has been re-arranged with glass from other windows.

The chancel stalls have an entertaining set of miserichords with the Labours of the Months, and other such subjects as four rats hunting a cat and sick man and his doctor. The 15th century tiles on the screen walls are the only ones of their type in England with about ninety different designs. Also in the chancel is an effigy of a knight of c1240 and a tomb with alabaster effigies of John Knottesford, d1589, and his wife.

GREAT WHITLEY   *St Michael*   SO 769650

This remarkable church beside a large ruined mansion was built for Thomas Foley, created Lord Foley in 1712. It was consecrated three years after his death in 1732. The building is a plain rectangle of three bays by five with slight projections set either side of the shallow chancel, and a west tower which does not project externally. Originally the exterior was of brick with stone dressings but c1860 Samuel Dawkes encased it with ashlar. The interior, all white and gold, is amongst the best of its period in Britain. The ceiling paintings by Antonio Bellucci were originally executed for the chapel of the Duke of Chandos at Edgware c1713-20 and were purchased by the 2nd Lord Foley c1750, as was the stained glass of 1719-21 made by Joshua Price to designs by Francisco Slater. There is a huge monument by Rysbrack to the 1st Lord Foley, and also a tablet to Thomas Foley, d1677.

GRIMLEY *St Bartholomew* SO 836607

The west tower, the three bay north aisle, and much else, all date from 1886, but the nave south wall and projecting doorway are 12th century, the refaced chancel is of c1200, and the east and nave south windows (with some old glass) are 15th century.

HADZOR *St John The Baptist* SO 916625

The small nave and chancel are both of c1300 but were very heavily restored in 1835 and 1866. A tiny porch tower was then added at the west end. The church is now a storeroom. It contains tablets to the Galton and Amphlett families.

HAGLEY *St John The Baptist* SO 921808

Parts of the south aisle and south arcade piers are late 13th century. A wide north aisle was added in 1826. The rest is work of 1858-65 by Street, who is said to have lengthened the nave by one bay. He replaced a chancel of 1754. In a partly original (but reset) recess in the north aisle is a fine foliated 13th century coffin lid. The urn with reliefs and the name Luciae is to Lucy, d1747, wife of the first Lord Lyttelton.

Hagley Church

Great Witley Church

HALESOWEN   *St John The Baptist*   SO 966836

The church is prominently positioned on a hill. It was originally a large 12th century cruciform structure with a central tower, transepts, and an aisled nave. Of it there remain the two western bays of each arcade, the west front with pilaster buttresses, the chancel and chancel arch, plus a south doorway reset c1300 when the south transept was swept away and a wide new south aisle and chapel and a south porch were built. The central tower collapsed in the 15th century and was then replaced by a new tower in a very unusual position in the middle of the original nave. This tower is joined to the chancel arch by two bays of 15th century arches. The north transept was then removed and a new aisle and chapel were built along the north side with between them a stair serving the loft over the Rood screen across the whole width of the church. In 1883 an outer south aisle of four bays was added east of the porch, and the NE vestry added. Inside the church are a large Norman font with a broad snake-like interlace pattern, a head of a churchyard cross carved with the Crucifixion, some old tiles, and a damaged coffin of a 14th century priest.

HALLOW   *St Philip and St James*   SO 828579

The best of several tablets in the church rebuilt in 1867-9 by Hopkins is a cartouche to John Pardoe, d1680.

HAMPTON   *St Andrew*   SP 029431

The unaisled nave, the central tower with a vault of eight ribs to a large circular hole for the bell-ropes, and the chancel all appear to be of c1400, whilst the stone-roofed south porch is slightly later. However, the chancel masonry and perhaps the priest's doorway are 13th century, there are Norman architectural fragments reset in the nave walls, and the north transept and vestry are 19th century. In the churchyard are a cross base with quatrefoils and fleurons and a monument with a sarcophagus to John Martin, d1717. See pages 7 & 10.

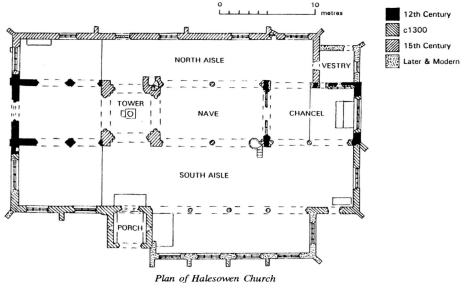

Plan of Halesowen Church

Hampton Lovett Church

Halesowen Church

HAMPTON LOVETT   *St Mary*   SO 888655

The church has an interesting plan with a 14th century porch tower on the south side and on the north side is the spacious Packington chapel of c1560 flanking the chancel and the east bay of the nave. Both nave and chancel are Norman and there is a blocked original north doorway. The chancel was lengthened and given a new chancel arch in the 14th century, when the nave was provided with new windows. The chancel south windows are 15th century. The tomb chest of John Packington, d1551, and its recess were much repaired during the restoration of 1858-9, when the nave west wall was rebuilt. The large tablet to Dean Hammond, d1660, is by Joshua Marshall, and the reclining effigy of Sir John Packington, d1727 is by Joseph Rose.

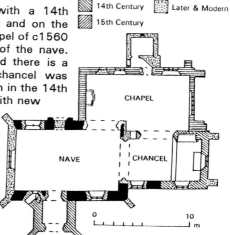

Plan of Hampton Lovett Church

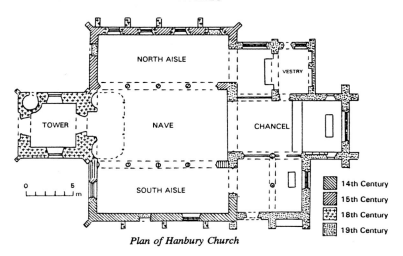

Plan of Hanbury Church

HANBURY   *St Mary*   SO 954644

The church lies alone on a hill with extensive views to the south. The arcades are of four bays and date from c1210 on the south and the 15th century on the north. The aisle walling may incorporate 14th and 15th century material but was rebuilt at about the same time as the addition of the large west tower in 1793. The chancel flanked by vestries on the north and a chapel on the south is of 1860-1 by Street. In the chancel is a monument with kneeling figures of Richard Vernon, d1627, and his wife. In the south chapel are large monuments with effigies of Thomas Vernon, d1722, by Edward Stanton, and Bowater Vernon, d1735, by Christopher Horsnaile.

HANLEY CASTLE   *St Mary*   SO 839419

The nave is Norman and the arch over the south doorway is original. To it c1300 was added a wide north aisle with a four bay arcade. Two south windows are also of c1300 and c1320 respectively. Of greater interest are the brick central tower, chancel and long north chapel, all of 1674, the year that appears on a plaque on the north side. The chapel windows are an interesting case of Gothic survival. The chancel windows and the north and south porch are Victorian.

HANLEY WILLIAM   *All Saints*   SO 673660

As originally built in the 12th century the church had a small nave and chancel originally separated by a very plain unmoulded arch on simple imposts. In the 13th century the nave was lengthened westwards and the old south doorway blocked and replaced by another further west. Four windows and the east buttresses are 19th century. The pulpit is a three sided screen cut from a single trunk of oak. See plan p7.

HARTLEBURY   *St James*   SO 841709

Of the old church there remain only the two bay arcade of c1300 to the north chapel, and the west tower which Bishop Sandys had built in 1587. Rickman rebuilt the chancel and its chapels in 1825 and the nave and aisles in 1836-7. A long thin west porch was later added in front of the tower. The font bowl lower half is Norman.

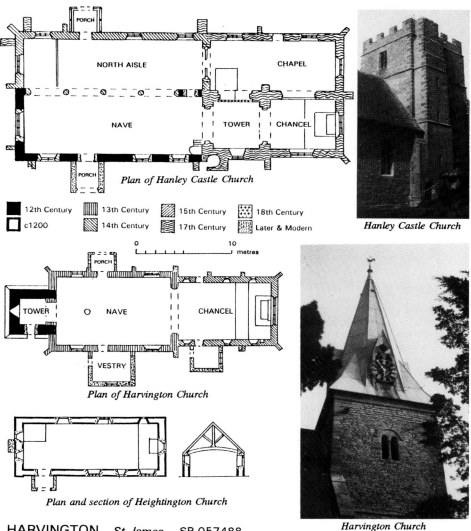

Plan of Hanley Castle Church

	12th Century		13th Century		15th Century		18th Century
	c1200		14th Century		17th Century		Later & Modern

Hanley Castle Church

0   10
metres

Plan of Harvington Church

Plan and section of Heightington Church

Harvington Church

HARVINGTON   *St James*   SP 057488

The Norman west tower has a tower-arch of c1200-10 and a spire of 1855. A wide new unaisled nave was built c1300, and the chancel with windows with unusual truncated ogival arches was built in the early 14th century. The north porch and chancel vestry are Victorian and there is a second vestry of 1961 beside the nave. There are tablets to Rector Thomas Ferryman, d1619, and his son Thomas, d1622.

HEIGHTINGTON   *St Giles*   SO 767712

The small window on the north side dates the single chamber to c1200. On the south side are 14th and 16th century windows. The very low interior has tie-beams.

HILL CROOME   *St Mary*   SO 888404

The short west tower and the nave and chancel are all probably 13th century. The chancel south wall flush with that of the nave suggests later widening, perhaps in the 16th century, the period of the unusual corner piscina. The communion rail, the pulpit and tester, and the font cover are all 17th century. See photo on page 12.

HIMBLETON   *St Mary Magdalene*   SO 946588

The oldest feature is the Late Norman south doorway. The chancel with a triple lancet east window is mid 13th century. Of the 14th century are the south transept and the timber framed south porch, whilst the weather-boarded bell-turret is probably 15th century. The north arcade and aisle are likely to be 16th century. There are good late medieval roofs over the nave and chancel. The Norman font has a small medallion with the Lamb and Cross. There is some old glass in the chancel and north aisle windows.

HINDLIP   *St James*   SO 879586

Except for part of the north wall, the 14th century single chamber was entirely rebuilt by Hopkins in 1864 and was given a south aisle in 1887. The west tower is 15th century but has 17th century belfry openings. It contains 15th century tiles.

HINTON-ON-THE-GREEN   *St Peter*   SP 025400

The masonry and north and south doorways of the nave are Norman. The doorways have columns and roll-moulded arches, and that on the north has a tympanun with an incised trellis. The font, the west tower, and the windows, gargoyles and battlements of the nave are all 15th century. The windows were given new tracery in 1865, the chancel was rebuilt in 1895, and the south porch is also 19th century. There is an incised slab of the 1490s depicting a priest.

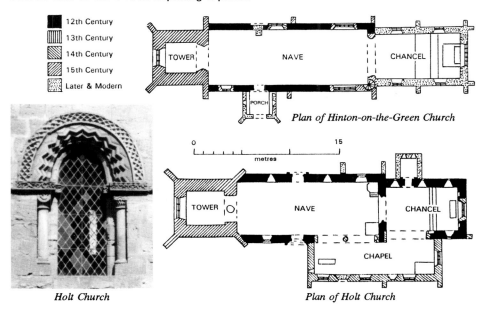

12th Century
13th Century
14th Century
15th Century
Later & Modern

TOWER   NAVE   CHANCEL   PORCH

Plan of Hinton-on-the-Green Church

0   15
metres

TOWER   NAVE   CHANCEL   CHAPEL

Holt Church   *Plan of Holt Church*

HOLT   *St Martin*   SO 829626

Both the nave and chancel are good examples of Norman work. Original are the chancel arch with scallop capitals on the shafts, a crenellation motif and chainlinks on the hood mould, several windows including one with shafts and an arch formed of chevrons, and the nave doorways. The south doorway has columns with capitals showing a man with foliage coming out of his mouth, a monster head, and chevrons on the arches. The font set below the arch of the 15th century tower is also Norman and has spiral fluting on the stem and monster heads with symmetrical trails on the bowl. The east window and the south chapel are 14th century. The position of the tiny west window of the chapel suggests a timber porch then existed. Opening from the chapel are two arches to the nave and a wider arch, probably later, to the chancel. In the chapel is some 15th century glass showing the Annunciation, a 15th century effigy of a lady, and a tablet to Mercy Bromley, d1704.

HUDDINGTON   *St James*   SO 943573

The church stands close to Huddington Court, and is reached across a lawn. The Norman nave has an original north window and a plain south doorway. One north window is of c1300. The short south aisle with a two bay arcade is 15th century and of c1500 are the timber north porch and the chancel. There are fragments of old glass in some of the windows, 15th century tiles in the south aisle, a Jacobean screen, stalls with linenfold panels of c1520, and a mid 17th century communion rail. There is a brass inscription to Adrian Fortescue, d1653, and also a marble monument to Sir George Wintour, d1658.

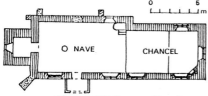

Plan of Hill Croome Church

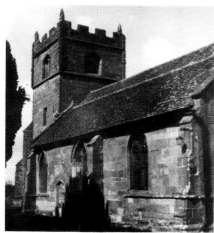

Holt Church

Plan of Hill Croome Church

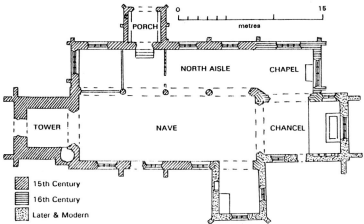

Plan of Inkberrow Church

INKBERROW   *St Peter*   SP 016572

The embattled north aisle with its four bay arcade and porch and the west tower are all of c1480-1500. The north chapel with uncusped tracery in the windows is early 16th century. In the 14th century south transept rebuilt in 1784 is a recently renovated alabaster monument of John Savage, d1631, and a tablet to Francis Sheldon, d1690. The chancel was rebuilt in 1887 by Ewan Christian. The square font of c1200 has dogtooth ornament on the underside and medallions on the side with a Lamb and Cross and rosettes. Several windows contain fragments of old glass.

Inkberrow Church

IPSLEY   *St Peter*   SP 066666

The four bay arcades, of the late 13th century on the south side and of the 15th century on the north, were blocked up when the aisles were demolished in 1785. Except for part of the east wall, the the chancel was rebuilt in the 19th century. The seven sided font with large ballflowers up the edges and crenellation is early 14th century, and the west tower is 15th century. The ornate Elizabethan pulpit was originally at Easton in Herefordshire. The wood relief showing the sacrifice of Isaac was probably made in the Netherlands in the 17th century. There are incised slabs to Nicholas Husband, d1553, and his wife, d1558, and Sir John Husband, d1583, and his wife, d1557.

KEMERTON   *St Nicholas*   SO 946347

The 13th century west tower has a west window, buttresses, and a top stage of the 16th century. The remainder of the church was rebuilt by Carpenter in 1847.

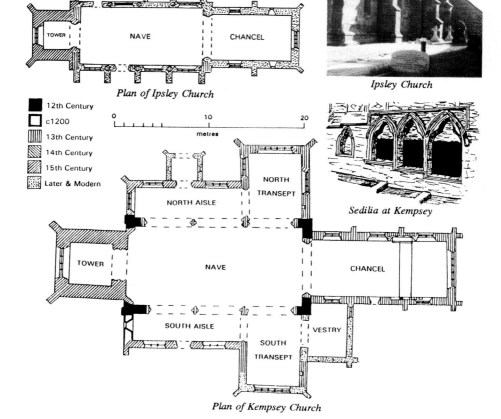

Ipsley Church

Plan of Ipsley Church

- 12th Century
- c1200
- 13th Century
- 14th Century
- 15th Century
- Later & Modern

Sedilia at Kempsey

Plan of Kempsey Church

KEMPSEY   *St Mary*   SO 848490

The corners still survive of a large unaisled Norman nave. By the end of the 12th century there was a south aisle of which the west window remains. In c1250-60 a splendid new chancel was built. It has pairs of lancets under blank arches and fine stepped lancets with internal shafting in the east wall. Shortly afterwards the south transept was added, and probably also the north transept, although its ogival headed piscina cannot be earlier than c1320. The arcades of three wide bays were built in c1300 and the west tower and several windows are 15th century. The south arcade arches are formed of alternate green and white stones. The Victorians added the north porch and rebuilt the chancel arch and the south transept end wall. The chancel windows contain good 14th century glass. Beside a shallow arch in the chancel north wall is a recumbent effigy of Sir Edmund Wydle, d1620. See plan on page 57.

KIDDERMINSTER   *St Mary*   SO 830769

This building has a quite exceptional length for a parish church on account of the formerly detached 16th century chantry chapel beyond the chancel. The chapel is rather plain and was refaced externally, like much of the church, in the 19th century. During that period were added the south chapel, the transeptal organ chamber, the cloister, and the vestry between the chancel and the chapel. The aisled nave is of six bays with the SW porch tower taking the place of the two western bays on the south side. These parts, with the fine clerestory, the chancel, and the three bay north chapel were all built between the 1480s and 1530s. In the north aisle is a fine brass of Sir John Phelip, d1415, and Walter Cooksey, d1407, and their wife with canopies above. In the south aisle is a buttressed recess containing a late 15th century female effigy. Set into recesses in the chancel are recumbent effigies of Sir Hugh Cokesay, d1445, and Thomas Blount, d1568, and their wives. In the south chapel are alabaster effigies of Sir Edward Blount, d1630, and his two wives.

Kidderminster Church

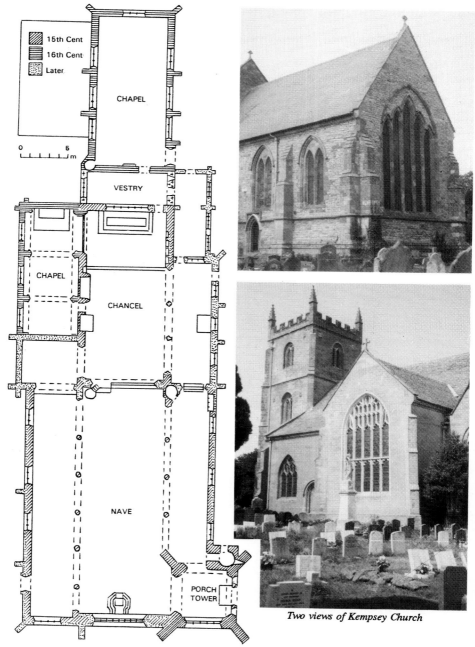

15th Cent
16th Cent
Later

0   5
m

CHAPEL

VESTRY

CHAPEL

CHANCEL

NAVE

PORCH
TOWER

Plan of Kidderminster Church

Two views of Kempsey Church

KINGTON   *St James*   SO 991559

The small 13th century nave and chancel formed a single rectangle until the nave was slightly widened to the south in the early 16th century. The chancel was mostly rebuilt in 1881. The western part of the nave and the timber framed bell turret are probably early 16th century. Decayed parts of the former screen are fixed to the south wall.

KNIGHTON-ON-TEME   *St Michael*   SO 634699

The eastern part of the nave with a projecting south doorway with colonettes, an arch with a roll-moulding and thin saltire crosses, and four blank arches above, and part of the thin south wall of the chancel are early 12th century. Later in the century the chancel was rebuilt and the nave extended westwards, this newer work having plinths whilst the older work does not. In the 13th century the nave was further extended to create a chamber supporting a shingled bell turret which was renewed in 1959. The nave and chancel each have a pair of windows of c1300 and the east window is Victorian. Fragments of old stained glass lie in a north window.

KNIGHTWICK   *Dedication Unknown*   SO 734561

A Norman font with chevrons lies in the chapel of 1879.

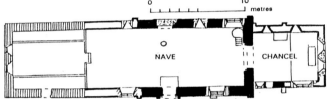

Plan of Knighton-on-Teme Church

Belfry at Kington

Knighton-on-Teme Church

Chancel at Leigh

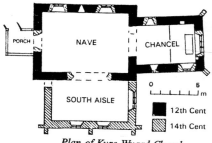

Plan of Kyre Wyard Church

Leigh Church

KYRE WYARD   *St Mary*   SO 626635

The church lies beside the mansion of Kyre Park (now a home for spastics) to which it is joined by a gallery. One north window indicates that the nave is Norman, and the chancel masonry is probably of the same period. The two bay south chapel with a wide single arch to the nave and an original wall painting of a female saint in a window embrasure is 14th century. Also of that period are several windows, the west doorway and probably the nave roof, but the bell turret carried on a beam at the west end is probably 17th century. There are black and white marble monuments to Edward and Catherine Pytts, d1672 and 1702. The bier is 17th century and there is an 18th century communion rail.

LEIGH   *St Eadburga*   SO 784534

The nave and the western two bays of the chancel with stepped pilasters are Norman. The four bay south arcade of c1190-1200 has round piers and pointed arches. The aisle was widened in the 13th century and its south wall was rebuilt in the 19th century. The chancel east end is late 13th century. The nave north windows and buttresses are of c1300 and the west tower is of c1380. It has a 15th century timber porch in front of it. The Norman font has a chevron band and scallops. In the aisle are 15th century tiles, a screen which was much repaired in 1855, and some old glass. In the chancel are tomb chests with recumbent effigies of Edmund Colles, d1606, and Walter Devereux, d1640, and the kneeling effigies of William Colles, d1615, and Essex Devereux, d1639, and their wives. The communion rail is probably 17th century.

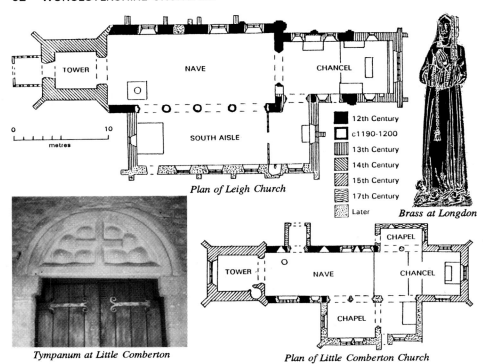

Plan of Leigh Church

12th Century
c1190-1200
13th Century
14th Century
15th Century
17th Century
Later

Brass at Longdon

Tympanum at Little Comberton

Plan of Little Comberton Church

LITTLE COMBERTON   *St Peter*   SO 967427

On the north side of the Norman nave are three original windows and a doorway with
a tympanum with a cross and four whorls on either side. The chancel and the tower
with a four centred arch are 15th century. The south chapel is Victorian but the tiny
north chapel is probably 17th century with a reset older east window and a Victorian
arcade. There are 15th century tiles in the chancel, there is some old glass in the SW
window, and also a Norman pillar piscina.

LITTLE MALVERN   *St Giles*   SO 777404

This church on a slope at the foot of the Malvern Hills originally served a Benedictine
priory. The Norman nave was destroyed after the Dissolution and a Victorian porch
now lies west of the central tower. The tower, the transepts, and the chancel were
rebuilt in the 14th century. Of the 1480s are the two bay side chapels with single
arches and squints towards the high altar, the chancel east window including its glass,
the panelled upper stage of the tower, the screen, the chancel tiles, and the stalls now
lacking their miserichords. The chapels and transepts are now ruined and the arches
to them are blocked up. Also blocked are the small doorways flanking the east window
which must have led to vestries or a former east chapel as at Great Malvern.

LITTLE WHITLEY   *St Michael*   SO 783635

Except for the 13th century north doorway, the church was entirely rebuilt on the old
foundations by Perkins in 1867.

Little Comberton Church

Little Malvern Church

LONGDON   *St Mary*   SO 837363

The west tower with Y-tracery and transoms in the belfry windows is of c1300. The nave was rebuilt c1786 and has shallow projections in the middle of each side, that on the south having a Venetian window. The short chancel, the apse, vestry and south porch are additions of 1868. There are brasses to William Bridges, d1523, and his wife.

Longdon Church

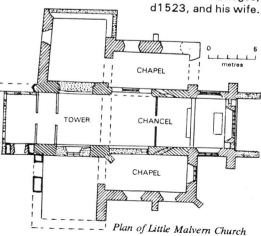

Plan of Little Malvern Church

Lower Sapey Church

LOWER SAPEY   *St Bartholomew*   SO 699601

This derelict Norman church lies by a farm at the end of a lane 1.5km SE of the new church of 1877. Original are three original doorways and three windows. Other windows date from the 14th century.

LULSLEY   *St Giles*   SO 745554

The church of 1892-3 is now used as a house. The 17th century font and communion rail and a 12th century relief of a man have been removed to other churches.

MAMBLE   *St John The Baptist*   SO 688716

Except for timber south porch the church looks all Victorian from the SE. In fact only the SE vestry, the chancel east window, and most of the nave north wall are of that period. The nave, the three bay arcade and the west wall of the south aisle, the chancel, and the western chamber supporting a timber belfry are all of c1200. The aisle has windows, buttresses, a doorway, and an ogee-arched tomb recess of c1320-30, and of about the same period is the stained glass Crucifixion in the east window. In the tomb recess is a recumbent skeleton removed from the tomb chest of Thomas Blount, d1561, which lies in an arch towards brick north chapel that he added and which is now roofless. There is also a late 13th century effigy of a cross-legged knight wearing his helmet and with his arms lying down by his sides (an unusual pose). There are brasses to John Blount and his wife, d1510.

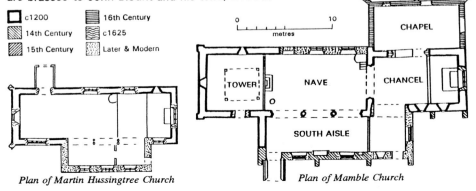

☐ c1200	▤ 16th Century
▨ 14th Century	▨ c1625
▨ 15th Century	▨ Later & Modern

Plan of Martin Hussingtree Church

Plan of Mamble Church

MARTIN HUSSINGTREE   *St Michael*   SO 877597

This is a single bodied church of c1200 with one original small window on the north side of the altar space. Several windows are 15th century, whilst the east and west windows, the north doorway, and the west buttresses are likely to be of 1625, the year once visible on a stone on the east gable. The three bay south aisle with reset older windows is an addition of 1883.

MARTLEY   *St Peter*   SO 756598

The wide nave with projecting north and south doorways with one order of columns is of c1140-50. The arches have rolls set between mouldings with small saltire crosses and lozenges. A new chancel as wide as the nave and having a roll-moulded priest's doorway was added c1200. The chapel containing the chantry founded c1315 has not survived but both nave and chancel have several windows of that period, and the single framed roof is probably also 14th century. The west tower with diagonal buttresses, battlements and corner pinnacles is 15th century. The nave has wall paintings of c1340 depicting what may be Christ's entry into Jerusalem and the Crucifixion on the north side, and the Annunciation on the south side (in which the Virgin is unusually placed on the left hand side). The chancel windows have painted patterns. There are old tiles in the chancel, and an alabaster effigy of a knight of c1460. The front of his tomb chest lies at the rectory.

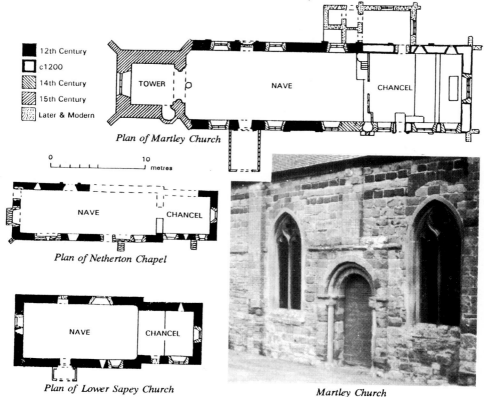

12th Century
c1200
14th Century
15th Century
Later & Modern

TOWER   NAVE   CHANCEL

Plan of Martley Church

0   10
metres

NAVE   CHANCEL

Plan of Netherton Chapel

NAVE   CHANCEL

Plan of Lower Sapey Church

Martley Church

Martley Church

Middle Littleton Church

MIDDLE LITTLETON

St Nicholas   SP 081470

The earliest features of the long nave are the 13th century north doorway and SW lancet, and the tower is also 13th century, with a 15th century upper stage. The north transept is of c1300, the south doorway and porch are probably late 14th century, and to the east of them is a small embattled chapel built by Thomas Smith, d1532. His brass within it has been lost. The chancel, chancel arch, transept and chapel arches, and several windows are Victorian. The Norman font has a band of thin lozenges. The pulpit has 15th century panels. There are late medieval bench ends, some traceried.

NAUNTON BEAUCHAMP

St Bartholomew   SO 963524

The small single bodied church was rebuilt in 1897 by Hopkins using some of the old material. The west tower is late 14th century, and the pulpit is of c1500. There are Jacobean communion rails and a long rhymed inscription on a tablet to Humphrey Lyttelton, d1624.

NETHERTON *Dedication Unknown* SO 990415

Beside Netherton farmhouse is a ruinous chapel with a long narrow late 12th century nave with original doorways. That on the north is the grander of the two, having columns and an arch with undercut chevrons with flowers, crenellation with triangular merlons, and elongated hexagons broken round an angle. The tympanum over the south doorway is earlier and probably not in its original position. There are also some late 13th century windows, and later alterations, including a fireplace in the west wall.

NEWLAND *St Leonard* SO 796485

A 13th century font ornamented with dog-tooth lies in the rebuilt church of 1862-4.

NORTH CLAINES *St John The Baptist* SO 851588

The outer north aisle and north porch were added by Aston Webb in 1886-7. Otherwise the church is all of c1480-1520 and comprises a west tower and a nave and chancel which are both fully aisled. Inside are a stone effigy of John Porter, d1577, a tablet to Mary Porter, d1688, and two other cartouches of c1693 and 1709.

NORTH PIDDLE

St Michael SO 968545

A 13th century bust corbel is re-used as a piscina in Henry Rowe's church of 1876.

Tympanum, Netherton

North Claines Church

Plan of North Claines Church

North Claines Church

NORTON   *St Egwin*   SP 043477

Much of the church, particularly the south wall, was rebuilt in 1844, when the vestry and porch were added. Prior to then the west half of the nave was roofless and divided off by a plaster partition. Two west lancets and some walling remain of the nave consecrated in 1295. The north transept is 14th century. Of the 15th century are the chancel and west tower with large lozenge shaped or round hoodmould stops to the windows, the large window from Bengeworth church on the north side and the font. There is early 16th century panelling in the chancel, and the pulpit is Jacobean. The limestone lectern is a fine piece of sculpture probably dating c1180-90. It was dug up in Evesham Abbey churchyard in 1813 and installed at Norton in 1865. There are recumbent effigies of Thomas Bigg, d1581, and his wife on a tomb chest, and of Sir Thomas Bigg, d1621, plus kneeling figures of Sir Thomas Bigg, d1613, and his wife.

NORTON-BY-KEMPSEY   *St James*   SO 877512

The Victorian four bay south aisle and east window have more impact visually than the Norman nave and chancel. There are two Norman doorways, that on the south reset, a Norman window, a 13th century north window, and a 15th century tower.

ODDINGLEY   *St James*   SO 915591

This small unaisled cruciform late 15th century church was heavily restored in 1851 by R.C. Hussey, the chancel being entirely rebuilt, although its windows and their glass are original. The nave was probably shortened when the 17th century tower was built. The arch to the south transept is of wood and has an opening for the stair to a loft over the former Rood screen. The window with intersecting tracery in the north transept is a reset piece of c1300, unless it is 17th century work imitating that era. The font may be 15th century, the communion rail is Jacobean, and there is an old hour glass stand for timing sermons now fixed on a front bench.

OFFENHAM   *St Mary and St Milburga*   SP 053463

Only the 15th century west tower and font survived the rebuilding of the church in 1861-2 by Preedy. The tower arch looks like a reset nave doorway.

OLD SWINFORD   *St Mary*   SO 908832

The 15th century west tower has now lost its spire. The nave was rebuilt in 1842 and the chancel was rebuilt in 1898.

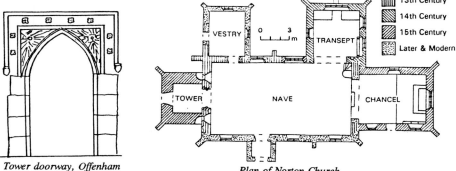

Tower doorway, Offenham   *Plan of Norton Church*

Old and new churches, Ombersley

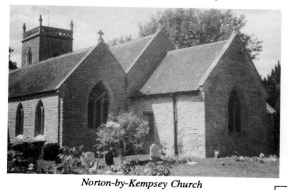

Norton-by-Kempsey Church

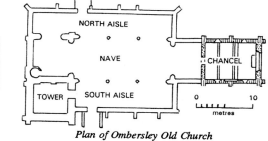

Old Swinford Church

Plan of Oddingley Church

Plan of Ombersley Old Church

OMBERSLEY   *St Andrew*   SO 844635

South of the ambitious new church built by Rickman in 1824-9 is the shortened (two bays instead of the original three) late 13th century chancel of the old church. It has been given new east and west walls and serves as the Sandys Mausoleum. Inside are a piscina and sedilia with trefoil heads and many monuments including a cartouche by W. Bird to Samuel Sandys, d1685. The old church had an aisled nave with three bay arcades, a west tower later replaced by a new SW tower, and a NW vestry.

OVERBURY   *St Faith*   SO 956368

The 13th century chancel has lancet windows and a rib vault. The east window dates from the 15th century when a new central tower replaced the original Norman one. The square headed and traceried belfry openings openings are 17th century and the vault is of 1880. The nave and aisles are Norman and have original 12th century windows set over the spandrels of the four bay arcades. The triple lancets in the nave west wall are 13th century. The north aisle has 14th century windows but the west and south outer walls were refaced in the 19th century when the south porch was added. The pulpit has parts from the 15th century screen and there are traceried panels on the bench ends. In the south aisle is a 13th century coffin lid.

PEBWORTH   *St Peter*   SP 128469

The chancel north wall is late 13th century but the east and south walls were rebuilt in the 15th century when the west tower was added. The nave north side and porch are 14th century and the south aisle with a three bay blocked arcade was built in c1510-20. The earlier window west of its blocked doorway must be reset. The font is 15th century, and the pulpit is Jacobean. There are tablets to two men both named Robert Martin who died in 1620 and 1720 respectively.

PEDMORE   *St Peter*   SO 912821

The present church is of 1871 except for the lower part of the tower, the Norman arch to the organ chamber which originally served as the chancel arch, the impressive Norman tympanum of Christ and the signs of the Evangelists above the inside of the south doorway, the trefoiled piscina, and the font which is probably Jacobean.

Pebworth Church

Pendock Church

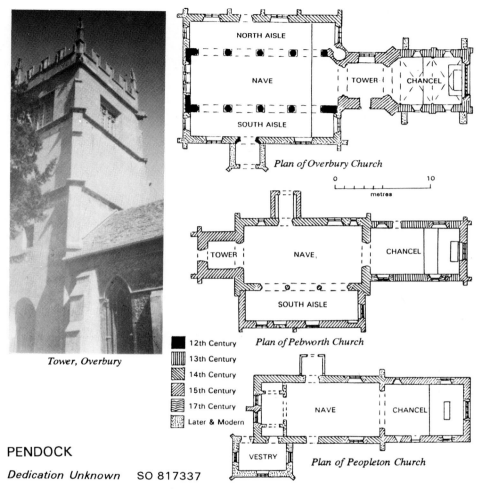

Tower, Overbury

NORTH AISLE

NAVE

TOWER

CHANCEL

SOUTH AISLE

Plan of Overbury Church

0 — metres — 10

TOWER

NAVE,

CHANCEL

SOUTH AISLE

Plan of Pebworth Church

■ 12th Century
▥ 13th Century
▨ 14th Century
▧ 15th Century
▤ 17th Century
▦ Later & Modern

NAVE

CHANCEL

VESTRY

Plan of Peopleton Church

PENDOCK

Dedication Unknown   SO 817337

The church lies in fields far from any village. Both the chancel and nave date from c1170 and the nave has original south and north doorways, the latter having columns and chevrons on the arch with a hoodmould with pellets. The chancel arch has probably been widened. One north window and the west tower are 14th century, two south windows and the timber porch are 15th century, and the chancel windows are 19th century. The dado remains of the medieval screen, the communion rail is Jacobean, and there are three 16th century benches.

PEOPLETON   *St Nicholas*   SO 937504

The nave and chancel have mostly 15th century features although the south doorway and masonry may be older, and the chancel windows may be 16th or 17th century. In the early 19th century a low brick tower was built around a timber bell turret at the west end. The SW vestry is late 19th century. The communion rail is mid 17th century, and there is a cartouche to Mark Dineley, d1682.

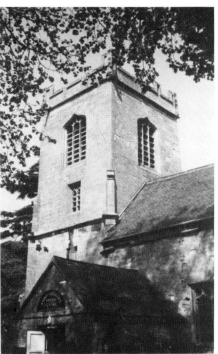

Pershore Abbey Church   *Former church of St Andrew at Pershore*

PERSHORE   *Holy Cross*   SO 947457

This is the remaining part of a church serving a Benedictine abbey originally founded c689 and rebuilt from c1100 onwards. The Norman nave was destroyed after the abbey was dissolved in 1539 and the north transept collapsed in 1689. The present chancel was built c1200-39 and was provided with new vaults soon after a fire in 1288. The crossing arches, now blocked up on the north and west, and the south transept with the usual pilaster buttresses and round headed windows are the only surviving parts of the Norman church. The very fine tower over the crossing arches is 14th century. The Norman font has Christ and the Apostles set under beaded intersecting arches, and trumpet scallop capitals against the shaft. In the south transept is a 15th century stone reredos and effigies of a cross-legged knight of c1280 and a 15th century priest. There are monuments of the late 16th and early 17th centuries to Thomas and Fulke Haslewood and their respective families.

PERSHORE   *St Andrew*   SO 948457

This was the original parish church of the town. It lies immediately east of the abbey church, which is now used for all services, thus allowing St Andrew's to be converted into a church hall. The north arcade of five bays dates from c1190-1200. Most of the rest is 15th century, having a wide south aisle with a slightly later tower at its west end. The brick south porch is early 19th century.

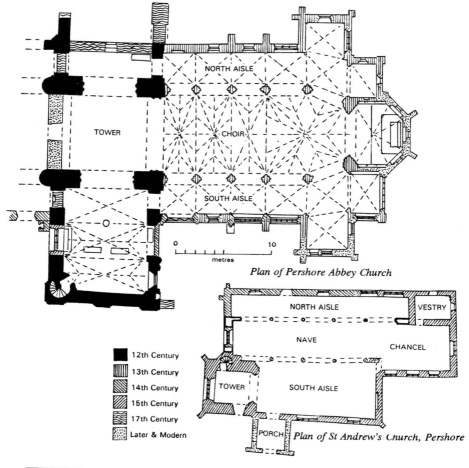

Plan of Pershore Abbey Church

- ■ 12th Century
- ▥ 13th Century
- ▨ 14th Century
- ▧ 15th Century
- ▤ 17th Century
- ▦ Later & Modern

Plan of St Andrew's Church, Pershore

Abbey church and former parish church at Pershore

Pirton Church

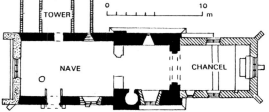

Plan of Pirton Church

■	12th Cent
▨	14th Cent
▤	16th Cent
▦	Later

PINVIN   *St Nicholas*   SO 957489

The nave is late 12th century and has of that period a south doorway, one north window and a font. The chancel is of uncertain date. The west end, the porch, vestry and all the other windows are Victorian, and the triangular bellcote is of 1884-5. The 13th century wall paintings on the nave south wall include the Adoration of The Magi and The Crucifixion. The pulpit includes the legs of an old communion table.

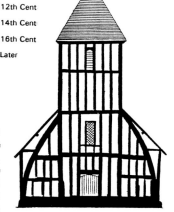

Pirton Church, The Tower

PIRTON   *St Peter*   SO 886468

As built in the 12th century the church had a comparatively short nave with a projecting south doorway with columns and chevrons, a central tower and a short chancel. In the 14th century a larger new chancel was built and in the late medieval period the tower top either fell or was taken down and a rare wooden framed tower with side aisles was built against the nave north wall. The south door was old ironwork and the communion rail is 18th century. The Pirton stone for casting pilgrims' badges has been taken to Oxford although there are reminders of it in the church.

POWICK   *St Peter and St Lawrence*   SO 834515

The transepts indicate that the church was already quite large by the end of the 12th century. They have long Late Norman windows and the remains of arches to former east chapels. A new chancel inclined to the north was built in the early 13th century. It has a triple east lancet and a pair of NE lancets, but the other windows go with the aisle outer walls and staircase to the Rood loft, which are early 14th century. The four bay arcades are of c1380-1400, and the tower with a panelled arch and the nearby font are 15th century. The oldest monument is that of Sir Daniel Tyas, d1673.

QUEENHILL   *St Nicholas*   SO 861366

The south doorway with columns, chevrons and a pellet hood-mould suggest a date of c1170 for the nave. Reset upside down in the refaced north wall is a Norman window head with two rosettes. The chancel was rebuilt in the late 13th century. One north window and the west tower are 14th century, and the east window is 15th century. Several other windows and the tower top with a saddleback roof are Victorian. The screen is 15th century. The pulpit is 17th century although it has a top band of older work probably from the former screen or its loft. One nave north window has a stained glass shield of arms of c1300.

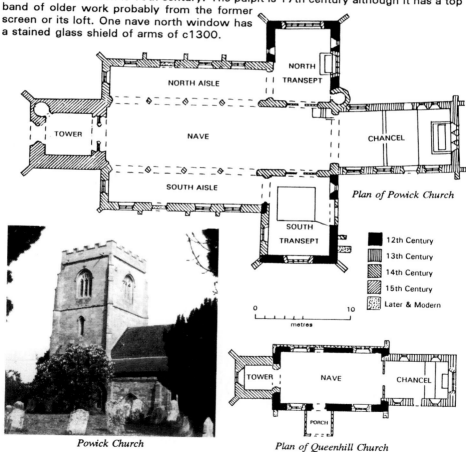

Plan of Powick Church

12th Century
13th Century
14th Century
15th Century
Later & Modern

Powick Church

Plan of Queenhill Church

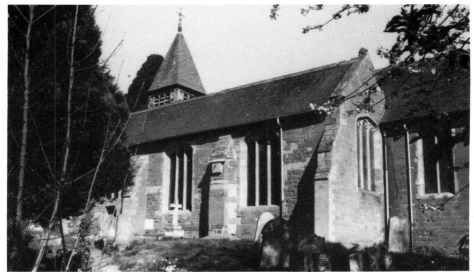

Ribbesford Church

RIBBESFORD   *St Leonard*   SO 787740

It would appear that what is now the west part of the north aisle served as the original Norman nave. It has a north doorway of that period with complex capitals with beaded interlace and there is a panel with a bird close by. The present nave built in the 15th century has a two bay arcade towards the old nave. The latter was extended eastward as a north chapel at about the same time and was given a new west wall in the early 16th century. A south aisle added to the nave in the late 15th century has a five bay arcade with wooden piers, the arches simply being curved braces. The church was badly damaged by lightening in 1877 and was restored in a way that caused much offense to Ruskin, the whole of the east end and the north chapel two bay arcade being of that period. Inside are various sculptured Norman stones from the lost chancel arch or the south doorway. The dado survives of the medieval screen. The pulpit is partly Jacobean. There are three coffin lids with crosses and there is a tablet to John Solly and his wife who died in 1639.

Ribbesford Church

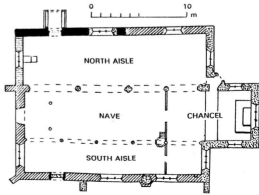

Plan of Ribbesford Church

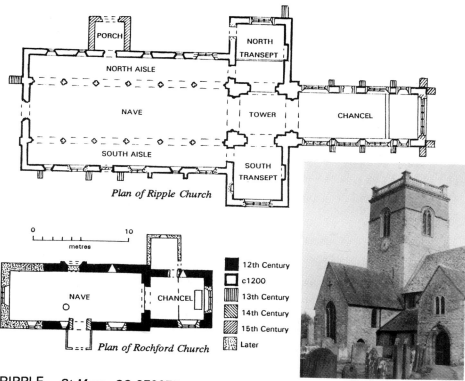

Plan of Ripple Church

0   10
metres

- 12th Century
- c1200
- 13th Century
- 14th Century
- 15th Century
- Later

Plan of Rochford Church

Ripple Church

RIPPLE   *St Mary*   SO 878377

This is quite a large cruciform church mostly of c1190-1230. The crossing arches, the transepts, and the chancel walling existed by 1200, whilst the nave with five bay arcades to comparatively narrow aisles is slightly later. There are lancets in the aisle outer walls and above the spandrels of the arcades and three original doorways, that to the west having three orders of columns. The chancel was remodelled at the end of the 13th century when the north transept end windows was inserted. The chancel east window and east corner buttresses, the north porch, and the upper parts of the tower are 15th century. The tower was heightened in 1713, and the top with a balustrade added in 1797. There was a spire until at least 1583, when it was hit by lightening. The porch was intended to be vaulted and carry an upper floor but the present upper storey is Georgian. The font with trefoiled blank pointed arches is of c1300 and there are stalls with some sixteen miserichords, twelve of which depict the labours of the months. The communion rail is Jacobean and there is old glass in a chancel south window. The oldest monument is the tablet to John Holt, d1734.

ROCHFORD   *St Michael*   SO 629685

The church lies near the River Teme. The west end, two windows, and the vestry are Victorian, and the south doorway and one window are 14th century. Otherwise the nave and chancel are all Norman work. The projecting north doorway has two orders of columns and a tympanum with a Tree of Life and an arched border of rosettes, all now very worn. The chancel arch has chevrons at an angle to the wall face.

Rock Church

Romsley Church

ROCK   *St Peter*   SO 732711

The nave and the western part of the chancel constitute the grandest Norman church in the county and were built c1160. There are pilaster buttresses, those at the corners projecting further and being stepped. The windows are placed high up above a string course and are shafted both inside and out. However they are rather oddly positioned externally with a blank window to the east of each, producing a rather unsatisfactory rhythm. The projecting north doorway has three orders of columns, an arch with chevrons, crenellation, lobes and thin rolls with a radiating three ray motif. The walls rise to a corbel table of heads. The many-shafted chancel arch with chevrons is particularly fine and has capitals with entwined shafts, a centaur, human heads and a boat. The chancel was given a new east window with reticulated tracery c1330, and its roof with tie-beams, collar-beams, and wind-braces may be of the same period.

In the south chapel are an incised slab to Richard Smith, rector, d1554, and a tomb chest with shields in quatrefoils. It is recorded that the tomb once had an inscription to Thomas Conyngsby which mentioned his son Humphrey as having built in 1510 the west tower, the south aisle with a four bay arcade, and the two bay south chapel. The font is Norman with nine rosettes connected by clasps, and there are various reset Norman fragments probably taken from the south doorway removed when the aisle was added. By the tower arch are the former village stocks and whipping post.

ROMSLEY   *St Kenelm*   SO 944807

The church lies high on the Clent Hills far to the west of the village. It is a single-cell Norman building constructed over a featureless crypt at the east end where the ground falls away. Near here, according to a disproved legend, a holy spring issued from the ground where St Kenelm was killed in 819. The south doorway of c1150 has two orders of columns and a tympanum showing Christ seated and crowned with angels holding his glory. The thick walling shows that the western part of the church is actually the base of a tower begun in the 1180s or 90s but with its upper parts demolished or never built. The present 15th century west turret of great charm is perched on an arch between two buttresses set against the older wall. The east wall of the church and the windows are all 14th century. High up on the south wall is a worn Norman figure of a saint, and on the chancel north wall is a 14th century painting with just one figure preserved.

Rock Church: north side

Rous Lench Church

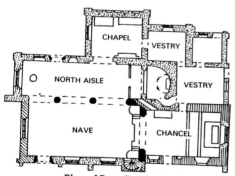

Plan of Rous Lench Church

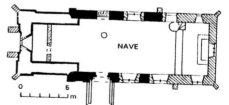

Plan of Romsley Church

ROUS LENCH *St Peter* SO 016533

The south doorway with chevrons and columns, the north doorway, the three bay north arcade, and the chancel arch are all late 12th century. Earlier, probably of c1140-50, is the very fine relief of a seated Christ high up on the south side. The nave was given a new west wall in the 14th century, and a stair turret to a roodloft was added on the south side in the 15th century. The south wall was otherwise rebuilt in the 19th century. In 1884 Preedy rebuilt the north aisle, added an apse at its east end with a series of vestries behind. He also added the north chapel in which are recumbent effigies on a tomb chest of Edward Rous, d1611, and his wife, d1580, a tomb chest without an effigy to Sir John Rous, d1465, tablets to Sir Thomas and Sir Edward Rous, d1676 and 1677 respectively, and a monument of 1719 to Frances Rous. The two Elizabethan pulpits have both come from other churches.

Interior of Rous Lench Church

RUSHOCK

St Michael

SO 884712

The church was built in 1758 by Roger Eykyn, probably altered c1800, and restored in 1872.

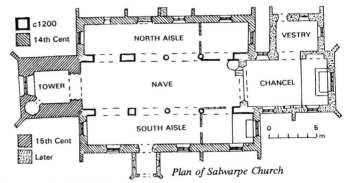

Plan of Salwarpe Church

SALWARPE   *St Michael*   SO 874620

The arrangement of the arcades of c1200 with three ordinary bays plus separate western arches on rectangular piers, and the evidence of a transverse arch which divided off the west bay of the north aisle, suggest that there was originally a NW tower. The present west tower is 15th century. The aisle outer walls with tomb recesses are 14th century but most of the windows are renewed. The chancel was rebuilt in 1848 but has round arched sedilia probably of c1530. There are 15th century tiles in the north aisle. In the chancel are a 14th century effigy of a priest holding a chalice, a tablet with kneeling figures of Thomas Talbot, d1613, and his wife, and in the south aisle is a 15th century screen and tablet to Olave Talbot, d1681, and a tomb chest to Olave and her mother Elizabeth, d1689.

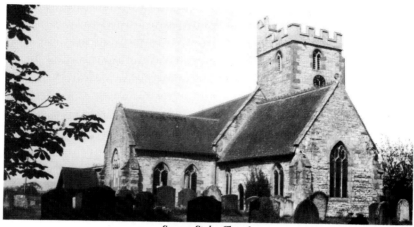

Severn Stoke Church

SEDGEBERROW *St Mary* SP 025385

This church, consecrated in 1331, but drastically remodelled in 1866-8 by Butterfield, has a wide single body of five bays. The small octagonal west tower is the chief original feature of interest. The vestry was added c1900. One north window contains 14th century glass depicting a seated saint. See photo on page 9.

SEVERN STOKE *St Denys* SO 856440

The large nave is Norman with clasping flat buttresses on the west corners, one north window high up, and part of a doorway arch reset on the north side. The north transeptal tower with a higher stair turret was begun c1300. Of the 14th century are the south transept and south aisle with an arcade of four bays in all, and the chancel and chancel arch. The east window has early Perpendicular tracery, whilst the transept east windows have recticulated tracery containing original glass. Beside the doorway are springers for the vault of an intended stone porch, the present porch being fairly modern and of wood. The font is 14th or 15th century and there are a few old tiles.

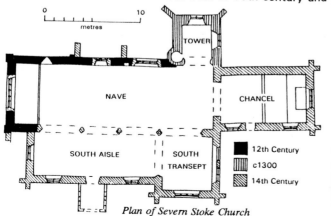

0 _____ 10
metres

TOWER

NAVE

CHANCEL

SOUTH AISLE   SOUTH
TRANSEPT

■ 12th Century
▦ c1300
▨ 14th Century

Plan of Severn Stoke Church

Tower at Severn Stoke

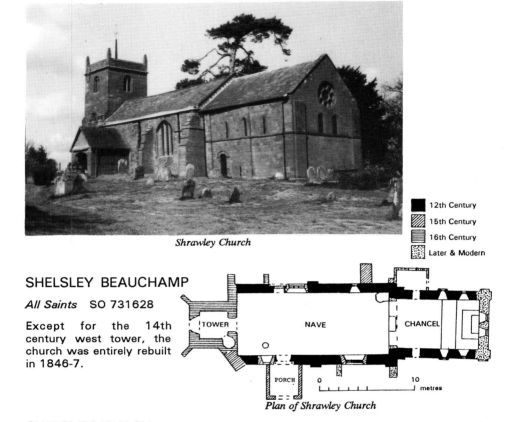

Shrawley Church

12th Century
15th Century
16th Century
Later & Modern

SHELSLEY BEAUCHAMP

All Saints SO 731628

Except for the 14th century west tower, the church was entirely rebuilt in 1846-7.

Plan of Shrawley Church

SHELSLEY WALSH *St Andrew* SO 722629

This is an attractive little church of tufa blocks. The nave is Norman and has several renewed windows and a north doorway with columns and chevrons on the arch. A plainer south doorway has been blocked up. The chancel is 13th century but its north wall was rebuilt in the 16th century and the external openings were renewed in the 19th century. It has a notable roof with tie-beams, collar-beams, and large foiled openings in the top triangle. There is also an original screen and parclose screen as a single composition, a rood beam, some 15th century tiles in the chancel, and a tomb chest to Francis Walsh, d1596.

SHRAWLEY *St Mary* SO 806648

The chancel is a fine structure of c1120-30. It has a sill frieze of chevrons on the south side and a rope on the north. Set on the sill are round headed windows, those in the middle piercing pilaster buttresses. The east wall and chancel arch are Victorian. Most of the nave was rebuilt c1180 and has north and south doorways of that date with columns and waterleaf and trumpet capitals respectively. One south window and the south porch are 15th century and the west tower is 16th century. The nave roof has fine old moulded beams.

SMETHWICK   *Old Church*   SP 021877

The church of 1778 is a brick building of four bays with a west tower. The earliest of several 18th century tablets inside is a Rococo cartouche of 1760.

SOUTH LITTLETON   *St Michael*   SP 081470

The nave has plain Norman north and south doorways and a NW window of c1200. A dedication is recorded in 1205. The SW window and the chancel with one original traceried window carved from a single block of stone are of c1280. The north transept is 14th century, the west tower and perhaps also the timber south porch are 15th century, and two south windows are 16th century. The tower arch is an earlier window head re-used. The east window and others, and the chancel arch, are Victorian. The round Norman font has a band of arrow heads and a rope band, three rosettes, and a cross. The pulpit, benches, and tiles in the chancel are late medieval. There is a defaced Norman pillar piscina, and a north window contains some old glass.

SPETCHLEY   *All Saints*   SO 896540

The church is now disused and has recently been repaired by the Redundant Churches Fund. It comprises a nave and chancel of c1330 with a tower probably of 1714 built into the west end of the nave, beyond which is a timber porch. The Berkeley chapel south of the chancel was built in 1614 but incorporates older windows. Set in an unusual bay window on the north side of the chancel is a late 16th century tomb chest to one of the Sheldons. In the arch between the chapel and chancel is the large and fine tomb with recumbent alabaster effigies of Rowland Berkeley, d1611, and his wife. Over the effigies is a coffered arch. In the chapel is an effigy of Sergeant Robert Berkeley, d1656, and a monument to Elizabeth Berkeley, d1708, and her husband.

STANFORD-ON-TEME

St Mary   SO 703657

This is an ashlar-faced cruciform church built by James Rose in 1768-9 on a site high above the river. Inside is a fine alabaster monument with effigies of Sir Humphrey Salway, d1493, and wife, and a standing monument to Thomas Winnington, d1746. See page 16.

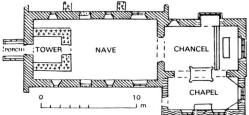

Shelsley Walsh Church

■ 12th Century	▧ 17th Century	▦ 18th Century
▥ 13th Century	▤ 16th Century	▨ Later & Modern
▨ 14th Century		

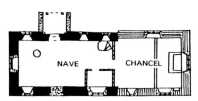

Plan of Shelsley Walsh Church

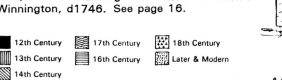

Plan of Spetchley Church

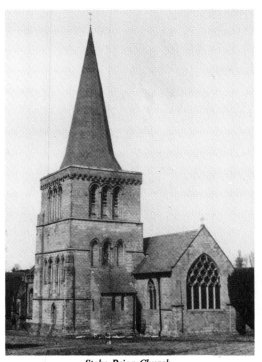

Stoke Prior Church

Wooden Tomb in Stockton-on-Teme Church

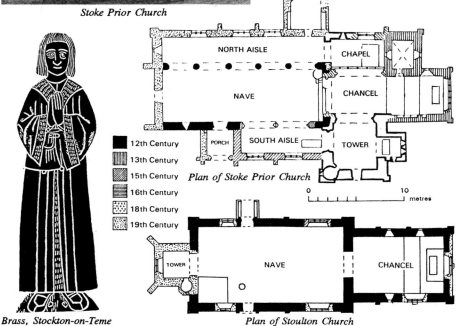

Brass, Stockton-on-Teme

12th Century
13th Century
15th Century
16th Century
18th Century
19th Century

Plan of Stoke Prior Church

Plan of Stoulton Church

STOCKTON-ON-TEME *St Andrew* SO 716673

The Norman nave of c1130-40 has a south doorway with columns and an arch with a roll and thin saltire crosses. The narrow original chancel arch now opens into a brick chancel of 1718. Several nave windows and the east window are Victorian. By the chancel arch are small Norman panels with the Lamb and Cross and a lion. There are 15th century tiles in the chancel. A 13th century coffin lid with a cross and a Lombardic inscription commemorates a former rector called Randulph. There is a small brass to William Parker, d1508, and there is a rustic wooden tomb chest to Thomas Walshe, d1593.

STOKE BLISS *St Peter* SO 652628

The nave north wall is probably Norman, like the font. The 13th century chancel has two south lancets. The narrow south aisle and arcade are of later in that century. The fourth or western bay of the aisle is now replaced by a porch tower of 1854, and the nave west wall, the vestry, and many windows are also of that date. There is one original window of note set in a cross gable on the south side. The screen is 15th century and the pulpit and reading desk are dated 1631 and 1635 respectively.

STOKE PRIOR *St Michael* SO 949677

The nave with a shafted south doorway and the five bay north arcade are of the last decade of the 12th century. Of the beginning of the 13th century are the narrow chancel, the north vestry, and the particularly fine transeptal south tower. The tower base served as a Lady Chapel with an altar set in a tunnel vaulted recess projecting from the east wall. The tower upper stages have blank shafted windows set either side of the real ones. The two bay south arcade is of c1250 but the aisle itself was rebuilt and given battlements and pinnacles in the 15th century. The chapel of St Catherine on the north side of the chancel has a west arch and one small window of the 1190s. In the 14th century the chapel was extended to meet the vestry west wall and given a new arch towards the chancel, and the chancel east window with recticulated tracery was also then inserted. The north aisle was entirely rebuilt in the 19th century and the vestry beyond and the south porch are also Victorian.

The 15th century font has angels holding shields. In the south aisle is a 13th century stone effigy of a priest and a brass plate to Henry Smith, d1606. Almost hidden behind the organ in the north chapel is a brass plate to Robert Smith, d1609.

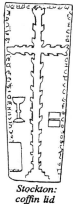

*Stockton:
coffin lid*

Stoke Bliss Church

Stoulton Church

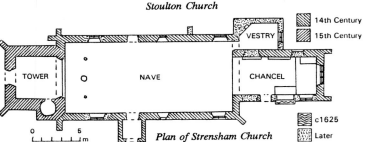

14th Century

15th Century

VESTRY

TOWER   NAVE   CHANCEL

c1625

Later

Plan of Strensham Church

*Russell Brass,
Strensham*

STOULTON   *St Edmund*   SO 906498

The wide and lofty nave and chancel of c1130-40 have many pilaster buttresses, original windows, and slightly projecting doorways, that on the south side having columns, a roll-moulded arch, and two bays of blank arcading. The chancel arch stands on simple imposts. The nave roof has arched braces up to collar-beams above which are two trefoils with a quatrefoil over. It is probably 14th century. The Norman font has a wavy top band. The west tower was rebuilt in 1936-7. In the church are a Jacobean communion rail, and a 15th century sword and helmet. There is old glass in a chancel south window.

STOURBRIDGE   *St Thomas*   SO 900841

The church is a large structure of brick with stone dressings built in 1728-36 and probably designed by the Parkers, a local family of masons. Its cramped setting in a back street is unfortunate. The four bay nave has round headed windows and a west tower with the parapet partly balustraded and curved up towards the corners. In 1890 the east apse was added, the eastern entrances were blocked, and it was probably also then that the tower was opened out towards the nave. Inside are Tuscan columns on high pedestals and a set of box pews dating from 1836. Nothing remains of the nearby chantry chapel of the Holy Trinity founded by the Harley family in 1430.

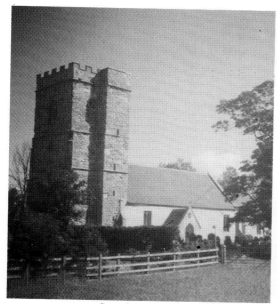

Strensham Church

Stourbridge Church

STRENSHAM   *St Philip & St James*   SO 911406

The wide nave and the narrow chancel seem to be mostly 14th century and the west tower is 15th century. The nave has a coved roof with tie-beams. The Norman font is decorated with arcading. The west gallery has painted saints of c1490-1500 from the former screen. There are 15th century tiles, 16th century benches, and an 18th century two decker pulpit. Particularly notable are the monuments set in the chancel. There are good brasses showing Robert Russell, d1390, and John Russell, d1405, in armour. John has a surrounding canopy. Other brasses depict Robert Russell, d1502, and Sir John Russell, d1562, and their wives. There are recumbent alabaster effigies of Sir Thomas Russell, d1632, and his wife, standing monuments to Sir Francis Russell, d1705, and Anne Guise, d1734, and a tablet to Mrs Dauncey, d1733.

SUCKLEY   *St John the Baptist*   SO 721517

The church was entirely rebuilt in 1878-9 by Hopkins. Older relics are the Norman font with a chain of decorated lozenges, the 14th century recess with ballflower ornamentation in the chancel, parts of the pulpit, and several of the dozen memorial tablets gathered together under the tower.

TARDBIGGE   *St Bartholomew*   SO 996691

The nave and the west tower and spire with a Baroque bell stage with corner columns were built in 1777 by Francis Hiorn, and the chancel is of 1879-80. Inside are a very large tablet to Lady Mary Cookes, d1693, and a mutilated effigy of a knight.

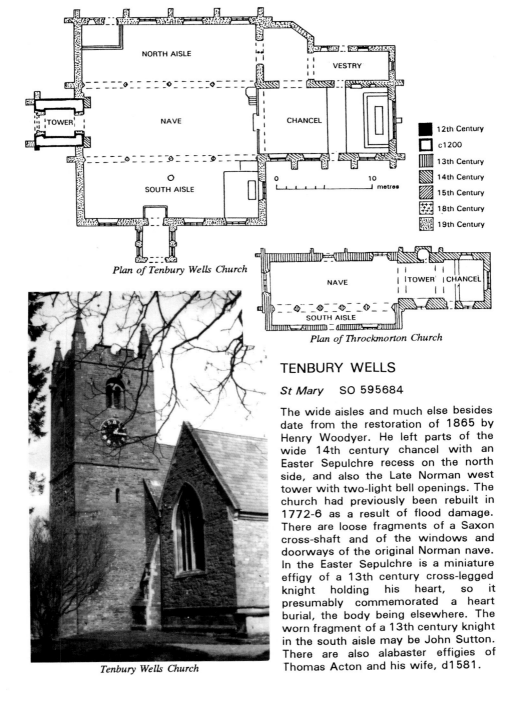

Plan of Tenbury Wells Church

12th Century
c1200
13th Century
14th Century
15th Century
18th Century
19th Century

Plan of Throckmorton Church

Tenbury Wells Church

TENBURY WELLS

St Mary   SO 595684

The wide aisles and much else besides date from the restoration of 1865 by Henry Woodyer. He left parts of the wide 14th century chancel with an Easter Sepulchre recess on the north side, and also the Late Norman west tower with two-light bell openings. The church had previously been rebuilt in 1772-6 as a result of flood damage. There are loose fragments of a Saxon cross-shaft and of the windows and doorways of the original Norman nave. In the Easter Sepulchre is a miniature effigy of a 13th century cross-legged knight holding his heart, so it presumably commemorated a heart burial, the body being elsewhere. The worn fragment of a 13th century knight in the south aisle may be John Sutton. There are also alabaster effigies of Thomas Acton and his wife, d1581.

Throckmorton Church

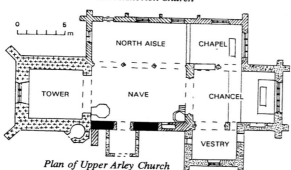

Plan of Upper Arley Church

The "Pepperpot" Upton-upon-Severn

THROCKMORTON *Dedication Unknown* SO 982499

The church lies in a field and has a very narrow 13th century south aisle with a five bay arcade. The middle arch, corresponding with the doorway, is lower and narrower than the others. The central tower, short chancel, and the west and north windows of the nave are all of c1300. The church was heavily restored in 1880.

UPPER ARLEY *St Peter* SO 764805

The modest Norman nave was given a three bay north aisle and a new chancel arch in the 14th century. The north chapel, the stair to the rood loft on the south side of the nave, and the clerestory are of c1500. The west tower has 18th century bell openings although the lower stage may be late 16th century on the site of a still older tower. In 1885 the chancel and south porch were rebuilt and the organ and vestry chamber added. The damaged 14th century effigy of a knight may be Sir Walter de Balun. There is a tablet to Sir Henry Lyttleton, d1693.

UPTON-UPON-SEVERN *St Peter and St Paul* SO 852408

The old church lies close to the bridge between the town and the river. It was entirely rebuilt in 1756-7 except for the west tower of c1300 furnished by Anthony Keck in 1769-70 with a notable octagonal top stage with a lantern (known locally as "the pepperpot"). The old church was abandoned after a new church was erected at the other end of the town and, except for the west tower, now used as a tourist information centre, it was demolished in 1937. A few foundations of it survive.

UPTON SNODSBURY   *St Kenelm*   SO 943544

The church was heavily restored in 1873-4 by Hopkins but retains a 15th century west tower, three 13th century lancets in the nave north wall, 14th century windows in the chancel, and a south aisle of c1500 with an original doorway and a four bay arcade of four-centred arches. Also of that period are the font with signs of the Evangelists in quatrefoil panels, parts of the screen, and cross-battened south door. In the chancel are fragments of old glass.

UPTON WARREN   *St Michael*   SO 931675

The transeptal south tower has roll-moulded belfry openings with plate tracery of c1260-70, but the tower arch, its windows, and the diagonal buttresses, are 14th century. The stone with the year 1664 may date the chancel masonry, although there was further building work there in 1724, whilst the nave was entirely rebuilt in 1798.

WARNDON   *St Nicholas*   SO 888569

The pebble dashed main body is Norman with a later east end. The timber north porch and several windows, some with fragments of old glass, are 15th century. The timber framed west tower is medieval but defies closer dating. It has closely spaced vertical timbers in the lower part of the west wall and curved braces above. In the church are box pews and a 17th century communion rail. In the vestry are some sculptured fragments said to have come from Worcester Cathedral.

Upton Snodsbury Church

WELLAND   *St James*   SO 797399

A tablet to Thomas Evans, d1761, lies in the church of 1875 by Hugall.

WHITE LADIES ASTON

St John Baptist   SO 923527

The north aisle, the west front, and much of the rest is of 1861-4, but the south doorway of the nave and the chancel windows are Norman. At the west end is a tall weatherboarded bell turret surmounted by a spire. The twelve sided font with rolls on the edges is of uncertain date.

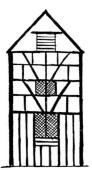

Warndon: Tower

White Ladies Aston Church

WICHENFORD *St Laurence* SO 787601

The south porch, vestry, spire, and most of the windows are 19th century, but the chancel is 13th century and the nave and the lower part of the tower are 14th century. In the nave is a tomb chest with recumbent effigies of John Washbourne, d1615, and his wife. In the chancel is a wooden standing monument of poor quality erected in 1632 to John's father John and grandfather Anthony.

WICK *St Bartholomew* SO 963454

The exterior looks mostly of 1861 and 1893 but the nave and chancel are both Norman with two original windows and a plain doorway. The blocked west arch may be Norman and probably once led into a tower. The three bay north arcade is perhaps Early Norman, but with the original round arches later made pointed. The communion rail with knobs is Jacobean, and the nave has a 15th century wagon roof. See p92.

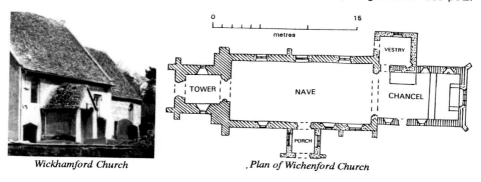

Wickhamford Church   *. Plan of Wichenford Church*

WICKHAMFORD   *St John The Baptist*   SP 068423

This delightfully unrestored church has a 13th century chancel with lancets in the side walls. The east window, chancel arch, and one nave window are 14th century. Another window is 15th century and several others, plus the south porch and west tower, are 17th century. Over the chancel arch is a 15th century beam with pretty cresting, above which is a tympanum with the arms of Charles II. The font, pulpit, and chancel have 17th century panelling. The pulpit stands above the lower part of a former three decker pulpit. There are box pews with 16th century linenfold panels, a gallery with three late 17th century carved panels from a London church, tracery panels under the tower, probably from a late medieval pulpit, and an 18th century communion rail. In the chancel are tomb chests with effigies of Samuel and Edward Sandys, both d1626, and their wives. See photo on page 17.

WOLVERLEY   *St John The Baptist*   SO 829793

This big red brick church comprising a west tower, nave, and chancel, was built in 1772 on a rock above the village. Inside are many 18th century tablets, a late 14th century effigy of a knight, and the tester of a pulpit of 1638.

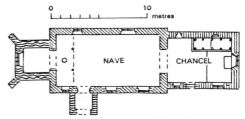

Plan of Wickhamford Church

Wickhamford Church

Wick Church

All Saints' Church, Worcester

Wolverley Church

WORCESTER   *All Saints*   SO 847589

Except for the 15th century lower stage of the large west tower, the whole church was rebuilt in 1739-42, probably to designs by Richard Squire. The top stage of the tower has paired pilasters. The aisled main body is six bays long with an extra bay for the altar, and there are coupled Doric pilasters outside. Tuscan columns are used for the arcades. Some windows contain fragments of old glass, the pulpit has 17th century panels, and the communion rail is 18th century. There are kneeling effigies of Edward Hurdman, d1621, and his wife, and many 17th and 18th century tablets.

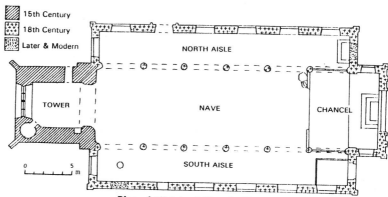

15th Century
18th Century
Later & Modern

NORTH AISLE

TOWER

NAVE

CHANCEL

SOUTH AISLE

0   5
m

Plan of All Saints' Church, Worcester

WORCESTER   *St Alban*   SO 849546

Although heavily restored in 1821 and later, this modest church is Norman, the three western arches of the arcade being of the end of that era. It now serves as a day centre for the homeless. Inside is a tablet to Edmund Wyatt, d1684.

WORCESTER   *St Andrew*   SO 848548

In 1779 the parish of St Andrew was the second most populous in Worcester but by the 19th century it was mostly full of warehouses. The church was eventually dismantled except for the 15th century west tower left standing as a landmark in a public garden. It has arches to the north, east, and south and a lierne vault. It rises 46m to the top of a slender recessed spire repaired or rebuilt seven times during the Georgian period when it was constantly being damaged by storms.

WORCESTER   *St Helen*   SO 850547

This church became a soldiers' club in 1939 and is now used as the County Record Office. It has 15th century arcades, but the west tower was rebuilt in 1813 and the aisle outer walls and east end (including the north chapel of 1288) were rebuilt in 1857 by Preedy. There is a standing monument with a figure of John Nash, d1662. A monument of c1600 to John and Anne Walgrave was long hidden behind the organ.

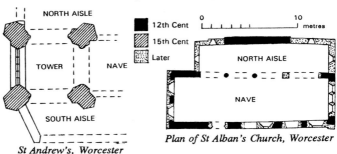

St Andrew's, Worcester

Plan of St Alban's Church, Worcester

St Andrew's, Worcester   *All Saints' Church Worcester*

Former church of St Alban at Worcester

WORCESTER   *St John*   SO 840544

This church in the suburb of Bedwardine west of the bridge has more medieval interest than most of the city centre churches despite the north aisle having been widened in 1841, and the chancel and north chapel having been rebuilt in 1884 by Ewan Christian. The round piers of the three bay north arcade are Late Norman, although the arches are renewed. The south arcade, chancel arch, south aisle (with renewed windows and later porch), and the west tower are 15th century. The south chapel and its two bay arcade and the arch for the original north chapel are 14th century. It was towards the end of that century that St John's was raised in status from a chapel to a parish church, and the original mother church of St Cuthbert at Lower Wick abandoned. Of it remain just a small bit of walling at Manor Farm. There are fragments of old glass in the chancel side windows, and a tablet to Abel Gower, d1669.

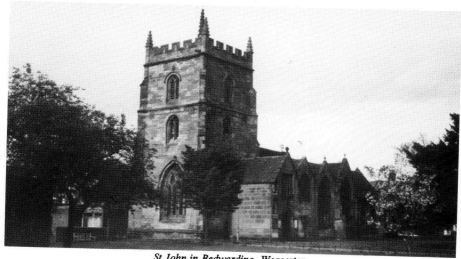

St John in Bedwardine, Worcester

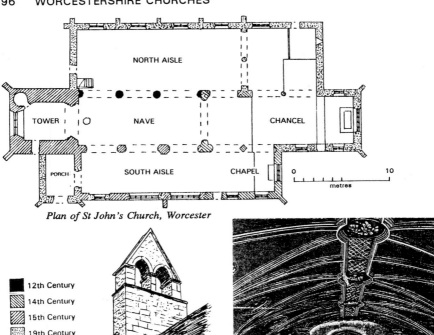

Plan of St John's Church, Worcester

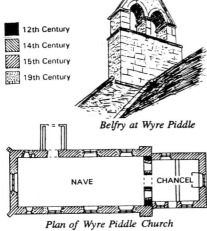

12th Century
14th Century
15th Century
19th Century

Belfry at Wyre Piddle

NORTH AISLE

TOWER   NAVE   CHANCEL

SOUTH AISLE   CHAPEL

PORCH

0   metres   10

NAVE   CHANCEL

Plan of Wyre Piddle Church

Interior of St Swithun's Church, Worcester

WORCESTER   *St Martin*   SO 851550

The medieval church had three gables on the south aisle and a timber south porch. Twenty trees were donated towards rebuilding the north aisle in 1616. The present church is of brick with stone details and was built at a cost of £2,215 in 1768-72 to a design by Anthony Keck. There are five bay aisles with Ionic Columns and groin vaults, but the nave is flat ceiled. The tower has balustrades and corner urns. The tracery in the east window was inserted in 1855-62. See photo on page 9.

WORCESTER   *St Nicholas*   SO 850550

This rectangular church with an east apse and a west tower embraced by two staircase bays was built in 1730-5 by Humphrey Hollins. The tower is based on a design by Gibbs published just two years before. It has stepped and recessed rounded corners and then an octagonal stage and a double curved cap and lantern.

WORCESTER   *St Swithun*   SO 850549

The church was rebuilt in 1734-6, probably to designs by the Woodwards of Chipping Campden. Each side has six narrow bays with big fluted Doric pilasters and windows with keyed-in round arches. The show front to the east has a richly decorated Venetian window and a broken pediment with a clock on top. The aisleless interior has a segmental vault with imitation gothic ribs. The west tower has ogee-headed belfry openings and is surmounted by balustrades and corner pinnacles.

WYCHBOLD   *St Mary*   SO 929658

The large church of 1888-9 built by Lewis Shepherd at the expense of John Corbett has a SE tower with an original late 13th century doorway and east window.

WYRE PIDDLE   *Dedication Unknown*   SO 962473

The plain narrow Early Norman chancel arch is flanked by openings probably of the 14th century. Above this wall is a 13th century double belfry. The nave masonry is late 14th or 15th century but the windows are Victorian. The Norman font has a band of vertical chevrons and another of ordinary chevrons. There is a Norman pillar piscina. In the west window are fragments of old glass and in the chancel are 15th century tiles. The two large animal heads loose in the vestry were probably corbels.

St Nicholas' Church, Worcester

St Swithun's Church, Worcester

OTHER ANGLICAN CHURCHES IN WORCESTERSHIRE

ASTWOOD BANK - St Matthias & St George - 1884 by Hopkins, nave rebuilt 1911.
BARNT GREEN - St Andrew - 19091-14 by A.S. Dixon.
BEARWOOD - St Mary - 1888 by J.A. Chatwin.
BENTLEY PAUNCEFOOT - St Mary - 1874-5.
BLACKHEATH - St Paul - 1869 by W.J. Hopkins.
BLAKEDOWN - St James - 1866 by G.E. Street.
BRADLEY - St John Baptist - 1864-5 by W.J. Hopkins.
BROADHEATH - Christchurch - 1903-4 by C. Ford Whitcombe.
BROADWAY - St Michael - 1839 by H. Eginton, restored 1890.
BROMSGROVE - All Saints 1872-4 by John Cotton, tower added 1888.
CATSHILL - Christ Church - 1838 by H. Eginton.
CHARLTON - St John Evangelist - 1872-3.
CHURCHILL - St James - 1868 by W.J. Hopkins.
COOKHILL - St Paul - 1876.
COOKLEY - St Peter - 1849 by E. Smith, enlarged 1872 by J.T. Meredith.
CRADLEY - St John - 1855-6 by F. Preedy.
CRADLEY - St Peter - 1789, tower 1876, apse 1933.
CRADLEY HEATH - St Luke - 1847 by William Bourne, apse added 1874.
CRADLEY HEATH - St Philip - 1893 by Alfred Pilkington.
DODDERHAM - St Mary - 1856 by A.E. Perkins.
DODFORD - Holy Trinity & St Mary - 1907-8 by Arthur Bartlett.
DOWLES - This church was demolished in the 1960s.
DROITWICH - St Nicholas - 1869 by John Smith.
DRAKE'S BROUGHTON - St Barnabas - 1857 by W.J. Hopkins.
FAIRFIELD - St Mary - 1854 by Benjamin Ferry.
FAR FOREST - Holy Trinity - 1844 by A.E. Perkins.
FINSTALL - Old Church - 1773.
FINSTALL - St Godwald - 1883-4 by John Cotton.
FRANCHE - St Barnabas - 1871 by Chamberlain & Martin.
GREAT WITLEY - St Michael - 1882 by Perkins, enlarged 1895, older font.
GUARLFORD - St Mary - 1843 by Thomas Bellamy.
HALESOWEN - St Margaret - 1907 by the Cutts brothers.
HANLEY CHILD - St Michael - 1807. Tower partly collapsed 1864.
HANLEY SWAN - St Gabriel - 1872-4 by Sir George Gilbert Scott.
HEADLESS CROSS - St Luke - 1867-8 by F. Preedy.
HOLLYBUSH - All Saints - 1869 by F. Preedy.
KIDDERMINSTER - St George - 1821-4 by Francis Goodwin. Interior 1924.
KIDDERMINSTER - St James - 1872 by Davis.
KIDDERMINSTER - St John - 1843 by G. Alexander, altered 1890-4 by J.A. Chatwin.
LANGLEY - Holy Trinity - 1852.
LANGLEY - St Michael - 1890-1.
LICKEY - Holy Trinity - 1856 by Henry Day.
LINDRIDGE - St Lawrence - 1861 by T. Nicholson.
LITTLE WITLEY - St Michael - 1867 by Perkins.
LOWER WYCHE - All Saints - 1903 by Nevinson & Newton.
MADRESFIELD - St Mary - 1866-7 by F. Preedy.
MALVERN - Christ Church - 1875-6 by T.D. Barry & Sons.
MALVERN - St Andrew - 1885 by Blomfield.
MALVERN - St Peter - 1863-6 by George Edmund Street.
MALVERN LINK - Ascension - 1903 by Sir Walter Tapper.
MALVERN LINK - Holy Trinity - 1850-1 by S. Dawkes, enlarged 1872.
MALVERN LINK - St Matthias - 1844-6 by G.G. Scott, altered 1880 and 1899.

MALVERN WELLS - St Peter - 1836 by Jearrad.
NEWLAND - St Leonard - 1862-4 by P.C. Hardwick.
OLDBURY - Christchurch - 1840 by Johnson, altered 1867.
OLD SWINFORD - St Mary - 1842-3 by Robert Ebbles.
ORLETON - St John Baptist - 1816.
PENSAX - St James - 1832-3 by Thomas Jones.
REDDITCH - St George - 1876-7 by F. Preedy.
REDDITCH - St Stephen - 1854-5 by H. Woodyer.
ROWLEY REGIS - St Giles - 1923 by A.S. Dixon & H.W. Hobbis.
RUBERY - St Chad - 1956-7 by Lavendar, Twentyman & Percy.
SMETHWICK - Holy Trinity - 1838, rebuilt 1887-8 by F.Bacon.
SMETHWICK - St Matthew - 1855 by Joseph James.
SMETHWICK - St Michael - 1892 by A.E. Street.
SMETHWICK - St Paul - mostly rebuilt 1965-6.
SMETHWICK - St Stephen - 1900-2 by F.T. Beck.
STAMBERMILL - St Mark - 1870 by J. Smith.
STONE - St Mary - 1831.
STOURBRIDGE - Christ Church, Lye - 1843.
STOURBRIDGE - St John - 1860 by G.E. Street.
STOURPORT - St Michael 1881-1910 to a design by the late Sir G.G. Scott.
TIBBERTON - St Peter ad Vincula - 1868 by Hopkins.
TRIMPLEY - Holy Trinity - 1844 by H. Eginton.
UPPER WYCHE - Good Shepherd - 1910.
UPTON-UPON-SEVERN - St Peter & St Paul - 1878 by Arthur Blomfield.
WEBHEATH - St Philip - 1869-70 by F. Preedy.
WELLAND - St James - 1875 by J.W. Hugall.
WEST MALVERN - St James - 1870-1 by G.E. Street.
WHITTINGTON - St Philip & St James - 1842 by A.E. Perkins.
WILDEN - All Saints - 1880 by W.J. Hopkins.
WOLLASTON - St James - 1860 by G. Bidlake.
WORCESTER - Holy Trinity, Shrub Hill - 1863-5 by Hopkins.
WORCESTER - Holy Trinity & St Matthew - 1964-5 by Maurice W. Jones.
WORCESTER - St Barnabas - 1884-5 by Ernest Day.
WORCESTER - St Clement - 1822-3 by Thomas Lee or Thomas Ingleman.
WORCESTER - St George - 1893-5 by Aston Webb.
WORCESTER - St Martin (London Road) -1903-11 by G.H. Fellowes Prynne.
WORCESTER - St Mary Magdalene - 1876-7 by F.W. Preedy.
WORCESTER - St Paul - 1885 by A.E. Street.
WORCESTER - St Peter The Great - 1836-8 by John Mills.
WORCESTER - St Stephen - 1861-2 by F. Preedy.
WRIBBENHALL - All Saints - 1878 by Arthur Blomfield.
WYTHALL - St Mary - 1862 by F. Preedy.

FURTHER READING

The Victoria County History of Worcestershire (4 vols).
Transactions of the Worcester Archeological Society.
Worcestershire (Buildings of England series) N. Pevsner, 1968.

A GLOSSARY OF ARCHITECTURAL TERMS

Apse	- Semi-circular or polygonal east end of a church containing an altar.
Ashlar	- Masonry of blocks with even faces and square edges.
Ballflower	- Globular flower of three petals enclosing ball. Current c1310-40.
Baroque	- A whimsical and odd form of the Classical architectural style.
Beakhead	- Decorative motif of bird or beast heads, often biting a roll moulding.
Broaches	- Sloping half pyramids adapting an octagonal spire to a square tower.
Chancel	- The eastern part of a church used by the clergy.
Chevron Ornament	- A Norman ornament with continuous Vs forming a zig-zag.
Clerestory	- An upper storey pierced by windows lighting the floor below.
Coffering	- Sunk square or polygonal panels on a ceiling.
Collar Beam	- A tie-beam used higher up near the apex of the roof.
Crossing Tower	- A tower built on four arches in the middle of a cruciform church.
Cruciform Church	- A cross-shaped church with transepts forming the arms of the cross.
Cusp	- A projecting point between the foils of a foiled Gothic arch.
Dado	- The decorative covering of the lower part of a wall or screen.
Dog Tooth	- Four centered stars placed diagonally and raised pyramidally.
Easter Sepulchre	- A recess in a chancel which received an effigy of Christ at Easter.
Elizabethan	- Of the time of Queen Elizabeth I (1558-1603).
Fan Vault	- Vault with fan-like patterns. In fashion from c1440 to 1530.
Foil	- A lobe formed by the cusping of a circle or arch.
Four Centred Arch	- A low, flattish arch with each curve drawn from two compass points.
Head Stops	- Heads of humans or beasts forming the ends of a hoodmould.
Herringbone masonry	- Courses of stones laid alternately sloping at 45 degrees to horizontal.
Hoodmould	- A projecting moulding above a lintel or arch to throw off water.
Impost	- A wall bracket, often moulded, to support the end of an arch.
Jacobean	- Of the time of King James I (1603-25).
Jamb	- The side of a doorway, window, or other opening.
King Post	- An upright timber connecting a tie-beam with a collar-beam.
Lancet	- A long and comparatively narrow window with a pointed head.
Lierne Vault	- A vault with a complex system of major and minor ribs and bosses.
Light	- A compartment of a window.
Lintel	- A horizontal stone or beam spanning an opening.
Low-side window	- A window with a low sill allowing those outside a chancel to see inside.
Miserichord	- Bracket underneath hinged choir stall seat to support standing person.
Mullion	- A vertical member dividing the lights of a window.
Nave	- The part of a church in which the congregation sits or stands.
Norman	- A division of English Romanesque architecture from 1066 to 1200.
Ogival Arch	- Arch of oriental origin with both convex and concave curves.
Pilaster	- Flat buttress or pier attached to a wall.
Piscina	- A stone basin used for rinsing out holy vessels after a mass.
Plinth	- The projecting base of a wall.
Queen Posts	- Two vertical timbers connecting a tie-beam and a collar-beam.
Quoins	- Dressed stones at the corners of a building.
Respond	- A half pier or column bonded into a wall and carrying an arch.
Reticulation	- Tracery with a net-like appearence. Current c1330-70.
Rococo	- The late phase of the Baroque style, current in mid 18th century.
Rood Screen	- A screen with a crucifix mounted on it between a nave and chancel.
Sedilia	- Seats for clergy (usually three) in the south wall of a chancel.
Spandrel	- The surface between two arches.
Tester	- A sounding board above a 17th or 18th century pulpit.
Tie-Beam	- A beam connecting the slopes of a roof at or near its foot.
Tracery	- The intersecting ribwork in the upper part of a later Gothic window.
Transom	- A horizontal member dividing the lights of a window.
Triptych	- Three surfaces, usually sculpted or painted, joined by hinges.
Tuscan	- An order of Classical architecture.
Tympanum	- The space between the lintel of a doorway and the arch above it.
Venetian Window	- Window with a square headed light on either side of an arched light.